HIT LIST
FOR
CHILDREN 2
Frequently Challenged Books

Beverley C. Becker
and
Susan M. Stan

for the

Office for Intellectual Freedom
of the
American Library Association

American Library Association
Chicago and London
2002

While extensive effort has gone into ensuring the reliability of information appearing in this book, the publisher makes no warranty, express or implied, on the accuracy or reliability of the information, and does not assume and hereby disclaims any liability to any person for any loss or damage caused by errors or omissions in this publication.

Printed on 60-pound white offset, a pH-neutral stock, and bound in 10-point coated cover stock by McNaughton & Gunn

The paper used in this publication meets the minimum requirements of American National Standard for Information Sciences—Permanence of Paper for Printed Library Materials, ANSI Z39.48-1992.∞

Library of Congress Cataloging-in-Publication Data
Becker, Beverley C.
    Hit list for children 2 : frequently challenged books / Beverley C. Becker and Susan M. Stan for the Office for Intellectual Freedom of the American Library Association.
        p. cm.
    Continues: Hit list : frequently challenged books for children / Donna Reidy Pistolis.
    Includes bibliographical references.
    ISBN 0-8389-0830-6 (alk. paper)
    1. Challenged books—United States—Bibliography. 2. Children's literature—Bibliography. I. Title: Hit list for children two. II. Stan, Susan. III. Pistolis, Donna Reidy. Hit list. IV. American Library Association. Office for Intellectual Freedom. V. Title.

Z1019 .B38 2002
098'.1--dc21   2002000905

Printed in the United States of America.

06   05   04   03   02   5   4   3   2   1

CONTENTS

ACKNOWLEDGMENTS

Special thanks to the Intellectual Freedom Committee of the Association for Library Service to Children, which was actively involved in preparing this edition. In particular, Carolyn Noah, chair of the committee, and Susan Stan, who did the lion's share of the work, were tremendously helpful.

PREFACE

Challenges to library and curricular materials are nothing new. Indeed, the ALA Office for Intellectual Freedom has received reports of more than 6,700 such attempts in the last ten years. There is no question that censorship attempts are increasing. Nevertheless, my rule of thumb—based on research—is that for every incident reported, there are as many as four or five that, for one reason or another, are not reported. So in terms of statistics, these numbers, distressing as they are, still represent only the tip of the iceberg. The prospect of a challenge, however, need not be feared or viewed with apprehension. In fact, some challenges actually prove to be valuable learning experiences for most of the parties involved.

It is my hope that this publication will assist you, whether this is your first challenge or your fiftieth. The books chosen for inclusion represent a broad range of children's books that have been challenged. For each title, the entry includes an annotation, examples of challenges, citations to reviews, articles about the book, and background articles about the book or the author, awards and prizes the book has won, where to look for more information on the author, and sources that have recommended the book.

Whatever the title that is being challenged, please remember you can always call the Office for Intellectual Freedom for assistance.

Judith F. Krug
Director
Office for Intellectual Freedom

The Stupids

Boston: Houghton Mifflin

In this series of four books, Harry Allard and James Marshall have created a fun-loving, witless family with a penchant for silliness. Readers meet them first in *The Stupids Step Out* (1974), in which the family of four goes on an outing that includes a window-shopping scene in which they mistake their own reflections for some "funny-looking people." In *The Stupids Have a Ball* (1984), Mr. and Mrs. Stupid throw a costume party to celebrate their children's achievement in flunking all their subjects in school, and Mr. Stupid attends as General George Washing Machine. *The Stupids Die* (1985) finds them in the dark when a fuse blows; they assume this means they're dead. When the lights come back on, they're convinced they are in heaven. *The Stupids Take Off* (1989) follows them on vacation as they visit numerous sets of relatives, all of whom live up to the Stupid name.

The books' humor depends on a combination of slapstick, puns, and downright nonsense conveyed through both the illustrations and the text. The pictures on the Stupids' walls, for instance, are mislabeled (a tree is identified as a flower, a boat as a car). Mrs. Stupid makes herself a new dress out of live chickens and then wonders if it is too loud ("cluck, cluck").

As Betsy Hearne observed in the *Bulletin of the Center for Children's Books,* these characters draw on a long tradition of fools in folklore. Leonard Marcus has described the Stupids as "a family of noodleheads whose talent for getting backward what every four-year-old can plainly understand is matched only by their boundless *joie de vivre.*" The first book in the series was greeted by *Library Journal* with a starred review, and the reviewer noted that "even youngest listeners will laugh with smug superiority as they follow these good-natured *dumbkopfs* from departure time to journey's end."

Both *The Stupids Step Out* and *The Stupids Have a Ball* were named SLJ Best Books of the Year. *The Stupids Have a Ball* was the International Reading Association (IRA) Children's Choice in 1979, and *The Stupids Die* was an IRA Children's Choice in 1982.

Challenges

Series

In 1993, the series was challenged by a parent in Horsham, Pennsylvania, who charged that the books undermine the authority of parents by making them look foolish. The books were removed and then returned to the school libraries in the district. In 1998, all four books were removed from the Howard Miller Library in Zeeland, Michigan, because of complaints that children shouldn't refer to anyone as "stupid."

The Stupids Step Out

Unsuccessfully challenged in 1985 by the parent of a first-grader in Vancouver, Washington, because it described families in a derogatory manner and might encourage children to disobey their parents. Also challenged in 1985 at the Cunningham Elementary School in Beloit, Wisconsin.

The Stupids Have a Ball

Challenged in 1993 by the parents of an elementary school child in Iowa City, Iowa, who felt it reinforced negative behavior and low self-esteem. Their petition to have it removed from the school libraries was denied by the school district committee.

Reviews

The Stupids Step Out

Booklist 70 (July 15, 1974): 1251.

Bulletin of the Center for Children's Books 28 (Nov. 1974): 37.

Kirkus Review 42 (April 1, 1974): 359.

Library Journal 99 (April 15, 1974): 1210.

The Stupids Have a Ball

Booklist 74 (March 15, 1978): 1185.

Bulletin of the Center for Children's Books 32 (Oct. 1978): 21.

School Library Journal 24 (April 1978): 65.

The Stupids Die

Booklist 77 (March 15, 1981): 1025.

Bulletin of the Center for Children's Books 34 (June 1981): 186.

Children's Book Review Service 9 (spring 1981): 101.

Horn Book 57 (Aug. 1981): 411.

School Library Journal 27 (Feb. 1981): 53.

The Stupids Take Off

Booklist 86 (Oct. 1, 1989): 277.

Bulletin of the Center for Children's Books 43 (Oct. 1989): 26.

Kirkus Reviews 57 (Nov. 1, 1989): 1600.

School Library Journal 35 (Oct. 1989): 72.

Series

Tisdale, Sallie. "The Real Happy Ending." *Utne Reader* 25 (Jan./Feb. 1988): 114–17.

References about the Author

Contemporary Authors. Detroit: Gale, 1985. v. 113, pp. 20–23.

Contemporary Authors, New Revision Series. Detroit: Gale, 1993. v. 38, pp. 15–17.

Something about the Author. Detroit: Gale, 1986. v. 42, pp. 23–28.

References about the Illustrator

Children's Literature Review. Detroit: Gale, 1990. v. 21, pp. 166–85.

Marcus, Leonard. "James Marshall." *Publishers Weekly* 236 (July 28, 1989): 202–3.

Something about the Author. Detroit: Gale, 1994. v. 75, pp. 125–30.

Sources Recommending These Books

Gillespie, John T., and Corinne J. Naden, eds. *Best Books for Children: Preschool through Grade Six.* 5th ed. New Providence, N.J.: R. R. Bowker, 1994.

Homa, Linda L. *The Elementary School Collection.* 22nd ed. Williamsport, Pa.: Brodart, 2000.

Blubber

New York: Dell, 1974

In this tale of peer pressure among suburban, well-to-do classmates, written by acclaimed author Judy Blume, Jill Brenner goes along with her classmates as they make fun of Linda Fischer, an overweight student. When Linda presents an oral report about whales and the uses of their blubber, Wendy, the group's ringleader, nicknames Linda "Blubber."

After Linda's report, Jill decides to be a flenser (one who strips blubber off whales) for Halloween. When Jill does not win the costume contest, she and her best friend, Tracy, go trick-or-treating armed with rotten eggs, silly string, and toilet paper. They break eggs into the mailbox of Mr. Machinist, and to prove it to Wendy, return to the scene, where Mr. Machinist is waiting with a camera.

As Jill's classmates continue to entertain themselves with lists of "how to have fun with Blubber," Mr. Machinist shows the families in the neighborhood the pictures he took Halloween night in order to identify the guilty parties. Jill and Tracy are caught and must admit they are sorry and rake leaves for Mr. Machinist.

To prove who told on Jill and Tracy, a mock trial is planned. When Linda isn't given a lawyer, Jill tells Wendy off and becomes the odd one out. Jill realizes she was acting mean not because she is mean, but because of the pressure of fitting in. Jill never learns that it is wrong to persecute someone; she simply learns that once the tables are turned, it hurts.

In its review, the *Bulletin of the Center for Children's Books* wrote, "A good family story as well as a school story, this had good characterization and dialogue, a vigorous first-person writing style, and—Judy Blume demonstrates again—a respectful and perceptive understanding of the anguished concerns of the pre-teen years."

Challenges

Removed from an elementary school in Arlington, Texas (1999), because educators objected to "verbal, physical, and sexual abuse of student upon student."

Banned at Clements High School in Athens, Alabama (1998), because of objections to two uses of the words "damn" and "bitch" in the novel. The decision was later reversed.

Because in the book "bad is never punished. Good never comes to the fore. Evil is triumphant," the book was challenged at the Perry Township, Ohio, elementary school libraries in 1991.

Challenged at the Muskego, Wisconsin, Elementary School (1986) because "the characters curse and the leader of the taunting (of an overweight girl) is never punished for her cruelty."

Challenged, but retained, in the Bozeman, Montana, school libraries (1985) because the book was deemed profane, immoral, and offensive.

Restricted at the Lindenwold, New Jersey, elementary school libraries (1984) because of "a problem with language."

Because of its strong sexual content and language, and alleged lack of social or literary value, the book was banned but later restricted to students with parental permission at the Peoria, Illinois, School District libraries in 1984.

Removed from the Hanover, Pennsylvania, School District's elementary and secondary libraries (1984) but later placed on a "restricted shelf" at middle-school libraries because the book was "indecent and inappropriate."

Reviews

Booklist 71 (Jan. 1, 1975): 459.

Bulletin of the Center for Children's Books 28 (May 1975): 142.

Kirkus Reviews 42 (Oct. 1, 1974): 1059.

Publishers Weekly 206 (Nov. 25, 1974): 45.

Reading Teacher 29 (Jan. 1976): 421.

School Librarian 28 (June 1980): 147.

School Library Journal 21 (Nov. 1974): 54.

Teacher 92 (March 1975): 112.

Background

Blume, Judy. *Letters to Judy: What Your Kids Wish They Could Tell You.* New York: Putnam, 1986.

Blume, Judy. "Tales of a Mother/Confessor." *Newsweek* 115 (summer/fall 1990): 18.

Bohning, Patricia, and Ann Keith Nauman. "Judy Blume: The Lady and the Legend." (bibliographical essay) *Emergency Librarian* 14 (Nov./Dec. 1986): 17–20.

"Censorship in Children's Books." (symposium) *Publishers Weekly* 232 (July 24, 1987): 108–11.

Merrill, Martha. "It's Still Judy Blume: Censorship in Alabama." (Alabama Library Association IFC survey) *Southeastern Librarian* 40 (winter 1990): 168–69.

Moe, Laura. "Who's Afraid of Judy Blume?" (why book banners target works of fiction; bibliographical essay) *Book Report* 11 (March/April 1993): 21.

Rice, Susan J. "I've Bought All the Judy Blume—Now What Do I Do? Book Selection for Young Adults." *Ohio Library Association Bulletin* 56 (April 1986): 22–24.

Awards and Prizes

Arizona Young Readers Award, 1977

North Dakota Children's Choice Award, 1983

Young Readers Choice Award, Pacific Northwest Library Association, 1977

References about the Author

Children's Literature Review. Detroit: Gale, 1976. v. 2, pp. 15–19.

Contemporary Authors. Detroit: Gale, 1978. v. 29–32, p. 72.

Contemporary Authors, New Revision Series. Detroit: Gale, 1992. v. 37, pp. 42–47; v. 13, pp. 59–62.

Contemporary Literary Criticism. Detroit: Gale, 1980. v. 30, p. 47.

Dictionary of Literary Biography. Detroit: Gale, 1986. v. 52, pp. 30–38.

Something about the Author. Detroit: Gale, 1995. v. 79, pp. 20–26; v. 31, pp. 28–34; v. 2, pp. 31–32.

Sources Recommending This Book

Colborn, Candy. *What Do Children Read Next? A Reader's Guide to Fiction for Children*. Detroit: Gale, 1994.

Gillespie, John T. *The Elementary School Paperback Collection*. Chicago: American Library Association, 1985.

Gillespie, John T. *The Junior High School Paperback Collection*. Chicago: American Library Association, 1985.

Gillespie, John T., and Christine Gilbert, eds. *Best Books for Children: Preschool through the Middle Grades*. 3rd ed. New York: R. R. Bowker, 1985.

Lee, Lauren K., ed. *The Elementary School Library Collection: A Guide to Books and Other Media*. 18th ed. Williamsport, Pa.: Brodart, 1992.

The Young Adult Reader's Adviser: The Best in Literature and Language Arts, Mathematics and Computer Science. Vol. 1. Ed. Myra Immell. New Providence, N.J.: R. R. Bowker, 1992.

Mommy Laid an Egg!
or, Where Do Babies Come From?

San Francisco: Chronicle, 1993

When Mom and Dad decide it's time to tell junior and his sister how babies are made, they go through a litany of explanations, from "sugar and spice and everything nice" (girls) to "slugs and snails and puppy dogs' tails" (boys). Babies, they explain, can be brought by dinosaurs, made out of gingerbread, found under stones, grown from seeds, or squeezed from tubes. In their own case, however, "Mommy laid an egg." The children think these explanations are hilarious, and they set their parents straight, explaining how seeds, tubes, and eggs *really* work to make babies. They illustrate their talk with stick-figure drawings, including "some ways mommies and daddies fit together." Such talk makes the parents blush, but the kids are perfectly at ease.

Cole's cartoon-like illustrations comically capture the nuances of life in a family where kids clearly rule the roost. Dad has a graying ponytail, Mom looks like an ex-hippie, and the house is filled with toys and pets. Unlike some informational books in disguise as stories, this picture book is truly entertaining while pulling no punches about the basics of human reproduction. In a starred review, *Publishers Weekly* called Cole's sense of humor "endearingly loony" and her drawings and text "candid without being offensive." Cole, who lives in England, has received numerous British awards, includ-ing the Kate Greenaway Medal in 1987 and the Kurt Mascher Award in 1996.

Challenges

In 1998, the mother of an eight-year-old girl who checked the book out of the Camden County Library in Missouri objected to the book. The library board subsequently decided to move it and all other books dealing with sex education from the children's section to the adult section.

Reviews

Booklist 89 (July 1993): 1969.

Children's Book Review Service 22 (Sept. 1993): 9.

Kirkus Reviews 61 (June 15, 1993): 783.

Publishers Weekly 240 (June 7, 1983): 78.

School Library Journal 43 (Jan. 1994): 104.

References about the Author

Contemporary Authors. Detroit: Gale, 1998. v. 161, pp. 77–81.

Twentieth-Century Children's Writers. 4th ed. Detroit: St. James Press, 1995, pp. 231–32.

Sources Recommending This Book

Gillespie, John T. *Best Books for Children: Preschool through Grade 6.* 6th ed. New York: R. R. Bowker, 1998.

The Goats

New York: Farrar, Straus and Giroux, 1987

At summer camp, Laura and Howie, who are social outcasts, are taken to a deserted island, stripped, and abandoned. Fearing further ridicule, they use a floating log to return to the mainland. They break into a locked summer cabin where they find food, clothes, and warmth, and call Laura's mother, asking her to come and take them away from this despicable situation. As a result of a major breakdown in communication between the two, Laura's mother insists that Laura stay at camp and try to adjust to the situation. Not wanting to return and face their horrid camp mates, Laura and Howie run away. In order to survive this physically and emotionally draining ordeal, they become burglars but do plan to pay everyone back for damages incurred. In their flight from the camp, the two encounter a group of youngsters from another camp who befriend them; a suspicious hotel cleaning lady who accuses them of indecent behavior; a kind old man who lends them money; and a mean, unpleasant deputy sheriff who finally arrests them.

This captivating novel explores many complex themes. A seemingly senseless but cruel prank has severe and far-reaching consequences on the lives of Howie, Laura, and her mother, Maddy. Howie and Laura experience extreme alienation from loved ones, peers, and adults. Because they believe that they only have each other, they begin to depend on each other and gradually gain each other's trust. As their intense relationship grows, Howie and Laura gain inner strength and feelings of self-confidence. By the end of the powerful, compelling novel, they have grown emotionally in many positive ways that enable them to move forward and overcome their status of goats—social outcasts.

Maddy also gains emotional insight from the incident. She realizes that she hasn't been the mother that Laura deserves and that she didn't handle the situation in the best way possible. Overall, her new-found concern for Laura's well-being and love for her daughter are evident at the novel's end.

This novel, written by an acclaimed writer and illustrator of picture books, was praised by many professional reviewers. *Horn Book* stated, "This novel by a welcome new voice promises to become a significant addition to the body of children's literature."

Booklist added, "Its many layers of concern, its relativity to today, its strength as a piece of writing, and its appeal for children mark this novel as one that will leave lingering echoes in readers' minds long after the story is over."

Anita Silvey, in an article that appeared in *Horn Book*, discussed the negative criticism. She wrote, "Critics of the book are concerned with the absence of positive adult characters—as was the case with

Harriet the Spy—and the change in the young protagonists from innocents to thieves. And all adult readers, I think, are disturbed by the raw emotion in the book—and the feelings brought forth from the reader."

Challenges

Challenged in Vigo County, Indiana, School District classrooms and libraries (1997) because the book is morally offensive and inappropriate for middle-school students. In November 1997, the Vigo County School Corporation committee affirmed that the novel is appropriate for use by middle- and high-school students in classrooms and libraries.

Challenged at the Timberland Regional Middle School in Plaistow, New Hampshire (1994), because parents said it contained "offensive and inappropriate" language for seventh-graders.

Because it contains a passage describing the rescue of a naked girl, the book was removed from the Housel Middle School library in Prosser, Washington, in 1992.

Reviews

Booklist 84 (Nov. 15, 1987): 564.

Bulletin of the Center for Children's Books 41 (Oct. 1987): 24.

Horn Book 64 (Jan. 1988): 68.

Kliatt Young Adult Paperback Book Guide 24 (Sept. 1990): 6.

New York Times Book Review 92 (Nov. 8, 1987): 31.

Publishers Weekly 237 (Jan. 1990): 112.

School Library Journal 34 (Nov. 1987): 113.

Voice of Youth Advocates 11 (April 1988): 22.

Articles about This Book

Campbell, Patty. "The Young Adult Perplex." *Wilson Library Bulletin* 62 (Jan. 1988): 75–76.

Silvey, Anita. "Editorial: *The Goats.*" *Horn Book* 64 (Jan. 1988): 23.

Background

Endicott, Alba Quinones. "Females Also Come of Age." *English Journal* 81 (April 1992): 42–47.

McDonnell, Christine. "New Voices, New Visions: Brock Cole." *Horn Book* 65 (Sept./Oct. 1989): 602–5.

Rochman, Hazel. "The YA Connection: *Celine:* A Talk with the Author." (Brock Cole) *Booklist* 86 (Oct. 15, 1989): 441.

Rochman, Hazel. "The YA Connection: *Celine*, Brock Cole, and Holden Caulfield." (significant new YA novel in the tradition of Salinger) *Booklist* 86 (Oct. 15, 1989): 440.

Awards and Prizes

Best Books for Young Adults, 1987

New York Times Notable Book, 1987

Notable Children's Book, 1987

References about the Author

Children's Literature Review. Detroit: Gale, 1989. v. 18, pp. 81–85.

Contemporary Authors. Detroit: Gale, 1992. v. 136, pp. 84–86.

Something about the Author. Detroit: Gale, 1993. v. 72, pp. 34–38.

Sources Recommending This Book

Carter, Betty, comp. "Teaching through Literature." *Booklist* 86 (May 1, 1990): 1996.

Children's Catalog. 16th ed. Ed. Juliette Yaakov. New York: H. W. Wilson, 1991.

Donavin, Denise Perry. *Best of the Best for Children.* Chicago: American Library Association, 1992.

Estes, Sally, ed. *Genre Favorites for Young Adults.* Chicago: American Library Association, 1993.

Estes, Sally, ed. *Growing Up Is Hard to Do.* Chicago: American Library Association, 1994.

Gillespie, John T., ed. *Best Books for Junior High Readers.* New Providence, N.J.: R. R. Bowker, 1991.

Gillespie, John T., and Corinne J. Naden, eds. *Best Books for Children: Preschool through Grade Six.* 5th ed. New Providence, N.J.: R. R. Bowker, 1994.

Junior High School Library Catalog. 16th ed. Ed. Juliette Yaakov. New York: H. W. Wilson, 1990.

Rochman, Hazel. *Against Borders: Promoting Books for a Multicultural World.* Chicago: American Library Association, 1993.

Scales, Pat, comp. "Children's Novels to Teach." *Booklist* 85 (Feb. 1, 1989): 944.

Zvirin, Stephanie. *The Best Years of Their Lives: A Resource Guide for Teenagers in Crisis.* Chicago: American Library Association, 1992.

My Brother Sam Is Dead

New York: Four Winds Press, 1974

Based upon actual events, *My Brother Sam Is Dead* tells the story of the Meeker family during the American Revolution. The story is told through the eyes of thirteen-year-old Tim, whose sixteen-year-old brother, Sam, leaves Yale to join the Continental army, and whose father is a marginal loyalist who doesn't want a war. Although Tim witnesses the conflict in his family, the war seems distant.

The reality of war hits Tim when he and his father make an annual trip to sell their cattle. It is the first time Tim has been allowed to accompany his father on the usually routine trip, and it opens his eyes to a new world. On the return trip, however, Tim's father is taken prisoner for selling beef that will feed British troops. When his father eventually dies on a British prison ship, Tim is left to run the family's tavern with his mother, who begins to sink into depression. Seeing his neighbors killed by British troops, and his brother unjustly accused and executed as a cattle thief by the Continental army, Tim avoids getting involved in the war. Years later, in his sixties, Tim reflects upon the war and wonders if there may have been another way to gain independence.

My Brother Sam Is Dead is a realistic depiction of the horrors of war and its effect on civilians; the authors vividly depict Tim's world. Because this is a book about war, the situations and characters are complex. The *Bulletin of the Center for Children's Books* wrote, "Well-paced, the story blends fact and fiction adroitly; the characterization is solid and the writing convincingly that of a young boy concerned more with his own problems and family in wartime than with issues or principles."

Challenges

Challenged in the Oak Brook, Illinois, Butler District 53 fifth-grade curriculum (2000) because of violence and inappropriate language.

Challenged as a gifted fifth-grade student assignment in Tucker-Capps Elementary School in Hampton, Virginia (1998), because the book uses "vulgar and profane language" and "contains scenes of graphic violence."

Challenged at the McSwain Elementary School in Staunton, Virginia (1998), because of "bad language."

Retained in the Antioch, California, elementary school libraries (1996) after a parent complained about the novel's profanity and violence.

Challenged in the Jefferson County Public Schools in Lakewood, Colorado (1996), because of "the persistent usage of profanity" in the book, as well as references to rape, drinking, and battlefield violence.

Because of profanity and violence, challenged, but retained, at the Palmyra,

Pennsylvania, area schools in 1994.

Removed from fifth-grade classes at Bryant Ranch Elementary School in the Placentia–Yorba Linda, California, Unified School District (1994) because "the book is not G-rated. Offensive language is offensive language. Graphic violence is graphic violence, no matter what the context."

Challenged at the Walnut Elementary School in Emporia, Kansas (1993), by parents who said that it contained profanity and graphic violence.

Because the book uses the names of God and Jesus in a "vain and profane manner along with inappropriate sexual references," the book was challenged in the Greenville County, South Carolina, schools in 1991.

Removed from the curriculum of fifth-grade classes in New Richmond, Ohio (1989), because the book contains the words "bastard," "goddamn," and "hell" and does not represent "acceptable ethical standards for fifth graders."

Reviews

Booklist 71 (Oct. 15, 1974): 241.

Bulletin of the Center for Children's Books 28 (March 1975): 108.

Horn Book 51 (April 1975): 152.

Library Journal 99 (Dec. 15, 1974): 3271.

Publishers Weekly 206 (Nov. 25, 1974): 45.

Awards and Prizes

American Book Award nomination, 1975

Jane Addams Peace Prize, 1975

National Book Award finalist, 1975

Newbery Medal Award Honor Book, 1975

Notable Children's Book, 1975

References about the Author

Children's Literature Review. Detroit: Gale, 1978. v. 3, pp. 44–49.

Contemporary Authors. Detroit: Gale, 1974. v. 9–12, p. 179.

Contemporary Authors, New Revision Series. Detroit: Gale, 1991. v. 33, pp. 92–94; v. 4, pp. 149–50.

Contemporary Literary Criticism. Detroit: Gale, 1984. v. 30, pp. 71–75.

Something about the Author. Detroit: Gale, 1993. v. 70, pp. 39–43; v. 8, pp. 33–34.

Sources Recommending This Book

Children's Catalog. 16th ed. Ed. Juliette Yaakov. New York: H. W. Wilson, 1991.

Colborn, Candy. *What Do Children Read Next? A Reader's Guide to Fiction for Children*. Detroit: Gale, 1994.

Cooper, Ilene, comp. "Past and Perilous: Historical Adventures." *Booklist* 86 (Jan. 1, 1990): 923–24.

Donavin, Denise Perry. *Best of the Best for Children*. Chicago: American Library Association, 1992.

Elleman, Barbara, and Ginny Moore Kruse, comps. "Contemporary Issues— Peace." *Booklist* 83 (April 15, 1987): 1299–1301.

Freeman, Judy. *Books Kids Will Sit Still For: The Complete Read-Aloud Guide*. 2nd ed. New York: R. R. Bowker, 1990.

Gillespie, John T., ed. *Best Books for Junior High Readers*. New Providence, N.J.: R. R. Bowker, 1991.

Gillespie, John T. *The Elementary School Paperback Collection*. Chicago: American Library Association, 1985.

Gillespie, John T. *The Junior High School Paperback Collection*. Chicago: American Library Association, 1985.

Gillespie, John T., and Christine Gilbert, eds. *Best Books for Children: Preschool through the Middle Grades*. 3rd ed. New York: R. R. Bowker, 1985.

Junior High School Library Catalog.16th ed. Ed. Juliette Yaakov. New York: H. W. Wilson, 1990.

Lee, Lauren K., ed. *The Elementary School Library Collection: A Guide to Books and Other Media*. 18th ed. Williamsport, Pa.: Brodart, 1992.

Middle and Junior High School Library Catalog. 7th ed. Ed. Ann Price and Juliette Yaakov. New York: H. W. Wilson, 1995.

"More Novels to Teach." *Booklist* 86 (March 1, 1990): 1354–55.

Shapiro, Lillian L., ed. *Fiction for Youth: A Guide to Recommended Books*. 2nd ed. New York: Neal-Schuman, 1986.

Weber, Rosemary. "Building a Children's Literature Collection: A Suggested Basic Collection of Children's Books, 1975 Supplement." *Choice* 12 (Nov. 1975): 1123–32.

Young Adult Reader's Adviser: The Best in Social Sciences, History, Science and Health. Vol. 2. Ed. Myra Immell. New Providence, N.J.: R. R. Bowker, 1992.

James and the Giant Peach

New York: Knopf, 1961

When James Henry Trotter's parents get eaten by an angry rhinoceros that has escaped from the London Zoo, he goes to live on top of a hill with his only living relatives—two mean, horrid aunts. James is expected to do all the chores around the house. He cannot play with other children. The aunts call him names, beat him, and deny him food. He is constantly punished for being a child. In spite of his abhorrent existence, James remains cheerful and optimistic about life and all that it has to offer him.

One day, the first of many peculiar things happens to James. He meets an old man who gives him a bag of magical and powerful tiny green things. In his excitement, James trips and falls, spilling the bag's contents all over the ground.

These green things cause a giant peach to grow on a usually barren peach tree. And much to James's surprise, five life-size, talking insects live inside the peach. James joins Miss Spider, Ladybug, Old-Green-Grasshopper, Earthworm, and Centipede in a marvelous, exciting journey as the giant peach and its inhabitants travel by land, sea, and air to New York City.

This whimsical, clever fantasy includes vivid scenes of death (James's parents getting eaten by a rhinoceros and his awful aunts being squashed by the giant peach), language that kids have always delighted in, and descriptions of the awful neglect James suffers while living with his dreadful aunts.

The novel's final message is positive. James experiences many hardships and copes with many difficult situations, but in the end he overcomes them all and has a rich, successful life, as do his traveling companions.

Challenges

Banned from the elementary school in Lufkin, Texas (1999), because it contains the word "ass."

Challenged at the Stafford County, Virginia, Schools (1995) because the tale contains crude language and encourages children to disobey their parents and other adults. The book was removed from classrooms and placed in the library, where access was restricted.

Challenged at the Morton Elementary School Library in Brooksville, Florida (1992), because the book contains a foul word and promotes drugs and whiskey.

Challenged at the Deep Creek Elementary School in Charlotte Harbor, Florida (1991), because it is "not appropriate reading material for young children."

Because the book uses the word "ass" and parts of the book deal with wine, tobacco, and snuff, the book was challenged at the Peterson Elementary School in Altoona, Wisconsin, in 1991.

Background

"Censorship in Children's Books."
(symposium) *Publishers Weekly* 232
(July 24, 1987): 108–11.

Colombo, Cristina. "Roald Dahl." (violence in children's literature) *Bookbird*
31 (Sept. 1993): 27.

Hitchens, Christopher. "The Grimmest
Tales." *Vanity Fair* 57 (Jan. 1994):
26–30.

Tisdale, Sallie. "The Real Happy Ending."
Utne Reader 25 (Jan./Feb. 1988):
114–17.

References about the Author

Children's Literature Review. Detroit:
Gale, 1984. v. 7, pp. 63–84; v. 1,
pp. 49–52.

*Contemporary Authors, New Revision
Series.* Detroit: Gale, 1992. v. 37,
pp. 123–28; v. 32, pp. 107–9; v. 6,
pp. 119–21.

Contemporary Literary Criticism. Detroit:
Gale, 1994. v. 79, pp. 177–82.

Something about the Author. Detroit:
Gale, 1993. v. 73, pp. 39–46; v. 26,
pp. 50–61; v. 1, p. 74.

Sources Recommending This Book

Children's Catalog. 16th ed. Ed. Juliette
Yaakov. New York: H. W Wilson,
1991.

Colborn, Candy. *What Do Children Read
Next? A Reader's Guide to Fiction for
Children.* Detroit: Gale, 1994.

Freeman, Judy. *Books Kids Will Sit Still
For: The Complete Read-Aloud Guide.*
2nd ed. New York: R. R. Bowker,
1990.

Gillespie, John T. *The Elementary School
Paperback Collection.* Chicago: American Library Association, 1985.

Gillespie, John T., and Christine Gilbert,
eds. *Best Books for Children: Preschool
through the Middle Grades.* 3rd ed.
New York: R. R. Bowker, 1985.

Lee, Lauren K., ed. *The Elementary
School Library Collection: A Guide to
Books and Other Media.* 18th ed.
Williamsport, Pa.: Brodart, 1992.

The Witches

New York: Farrar, Straus and Giroux, 1983

An orphaned boy and his eighty-six-year-old Norwegian grandmother make it their mission to rid the world of witches. The boy, narrator of the story, begins by passing on the information about witches that his grandmother has taught him: they always wear gloves to cover their clawlike hands, for instance, and they are good at passing for regular people, such as "your lovely school-teacher who is reading these words to you at this very moment."

Vacationing at a coastal town in England, the boy and his grandmother end up at the same hotel as the annual conference of English witches, who are posing as members of the Society for the Prevention of Cruelty to Children. The irony is obvious, since their mission is to destroy all children. The two happen upon the witches' plot and form a risky plan to overturn it. In the process the boy is turned into a field mouse—permanently. In any other book, readers could be sure that he would be returned to his human shape by the end of the story, but Dahl doesn't operate like that. Instead he resolves the tension by making the boy happy about his new form, since he can still talk, think, and act as a human and yet is free of the attendant responsibilities, such as going to school.

In a review for *School Library Journal*, Ellen Fader noted that "the author has crafted a special relationship between grandmother and grandson" and that "children will appreciate Dahl's honest way of dealing with death and separation." Comparing this book to Dahl's *The BFG*, the reviewer for *Horn Book* observed that "both books feature a narrator clearly allied with the young reader and two unlikely heroes who outwit evil on a grand scale." *Booklist* included the title in a list of books that will make readers laugh, calling it "one of Dahl's best" and "funny, but a little scary as well."

Challenges

Unsuccessfully challenged in 1998 by a parent in Dublin, Ohio, because it conflicted with her family's religious and moral beliefs. The school board voted to keep the book in the district's elementary libraries and retain it as a read-aloud selection in classrooms.

One of four books by Dahl to be retained in the Stafford County (Virginia) School District after a 1995 challenge by a parent, who was also a teacher and school board candidate in the district; she criticized Dahl's books because "the children misbehave and take retribution on the adults and there's never, ever a consequence for their actions."

The book's inclusion in the first-grade curriculum in Amana, Iowa, was challenged in 1987 by a parent who said the book was "too sophisticated and did not teach moral values"; the book was retained.

One of three books retained in elementary school libraries in Battle Creek, Michigan, by the school board after objection by a parent who felt the books were satanic.

Challenged in a Spencer, Wisconsin, fourth-grade classroom by a parent who felt the book could desensitize children to crimes related to witchcraft; school board voted to recommend continued use.

Unsuccessfully challenged in La Mesa–Spring Valley (California) School District in 1992.

Placed on a library restricted list by Escondido, California, Union Elementary School District in 1992 because of depicting witches as ordinary-looking women; removed from restricted list by school board members in 1993.

Challenged in the Dallas (Oregon) School District in 1991 by parents who felt the book could entice impressionable children into becoming involved in the occult; book was retained in elementary school libraries.

Challenged at Goose Lake, Iowa, Elementary School in 1990 because of alleged violence, use of the word "slut," the subject of witches, and the fact that "the boy who is turned into a mouse by the witches will have to stay a mouse for the rest of his life." The school Reconsideration Committee voted to keep the book both in the school libraries and in the curriculum without restriction.

Reviews

Booklist 16 (April 15, 1989): 1477.

Children's Literature in Education 19 (fall 1988): 143+.

Horn Book 60 (April 1984): 194–5.

Kirkus Reviews 51 (Nov. 1, 1983): J190.

Publishers Weekly 238 (Oct. 11, 1991): 64.

School Library Journal 30 (Jan. 1984): 74.

Background

Culley, Jonathon. "Roald Dahl—'It's about Children and It's for Children'—But Is It Suitable?" *Children's Literature in Education* 22 (1991): 59–73.

Dahl, Roald. *Boy: Tales of Childhood.* New York: Farrar, Straus and Giroux, 1984.

Hitchens, Christopher. "The Grimmest Tales." *Vanity Fair* (Jan. 1994): 26–30.

West, Mark I. Interview with Roald Dahl in *Trust Your Children: Voices against Censorship in Children's Literature.* New York: Neal-Schuman, 1988, pp. 71–76.

West, Mark I. *Roald Dahl.* New York: Twayne, 1992.

Awards and Prizes

New York Times Outstanding Book Award, 1983

West Australian Award, 1986

Whitbread Award, 1983 (U.K.)

References about the Author

Children's Literature Review. Detroit: Gale, 1997. v. 41, pp. 1–32.

Contemporary Authors, New Revision Series. Detroit: Gale, 1998. v. 62, pp. 111–18.

Something about the Author. Detroit: Gale, 1993. v. 73, pp. 39–46.

Sources Recommending This Book

Gillespie, John T. *Best Books for Children: Preschool through Grade Six.* 6th ed. New York: R. R. Bowker, 1998.

Guess What?

San Diego: Harcourt Brace Jovanovich, 1988

This easy picture book is a puzzle that is set forth on the front jacket flap: "Far away from here lives a crazy lady called Daisy O'Grady. She's got a secret. What could it be? Guess!" A series of increasingly descriptive yes-no questions, posed on one page and answered on the next, offers clues. Readers find out that she is tall and thin, wears a long black dress, likes animals, has a black cat, and, among other things, likes to fly at night on a broomstick. Yes, she's a witch, but a nice one, as evidenced by the last exchange: "Some people say she's really mean. But guess what? She's NOT!" The biggest clue to Daisy's identity is cleverly planted in the illustration on the jacket flap, where observant readers will find a street sign containing the silhouette of a witch.

Like Mem Fox's other books, this one is directed toward primary and preschool children and contains repetitive language and rhythm that invites children to participate in the telling. *Booklist* wrote, "Story hour participants will especially like the guessing game aspect of this story with its spooky surprises." The surrealistic illustrations, crammed with objects and precisely painted details, have received mixed response. The *Booklist* reviewer found it to be "some of the most exciting art seen in a children's book in a while," while *Publishers Weekly* considered it mismatched to the text and too sophisticated for the intended audience.

Challenges

In Libertyville, Illinois, a parent who felt that *Guess What?* was "not appropriate reading for young children" requested that the Cook Memorial Library remove the book from the children's department. The parent objected to the inclusion of witches, names of punk rockers, and other elements she inferred as negative in the illustrations.

Reviews

Booklist 87 (Sept. 1, 1990): 57.
Emergency Librarian 16 (March 1989): 25.
Kirkus Reviews 58 (Sept. 1, 1990): 1249.
Publishers Weekly 237 (Sept. 14, 1990): 123.

Background

Fox, Mem. *Dear Mem Fox, I Have Read All Your Books Even the Pathetic Ones (and Other Incidents in the Life of a Children's Book Author)*. San Diego: Harcourt Brace, 1992.

Fox, Mem. *Radical Reflections: Passionate Opinions about Teaching, Learning, and Living*. San Diego: Harcourt Brace, 1993.

Phelan, Carolyn. "Talking with Mem Fox." *Book Links* 2 (May 1993): 29–32.

References about the Author

Children's Literature Review. Detroit: Gale, 1991. v. 23, pp. 109–17.

Something about the Author. Detroit: Gale, 1988. v. 51, pp. 65–70.

Sources Recommending This Book

Gillespie, John T. *Best Books for Children Preschool through Grade Six.* 6th ed. New York: R. R. Bowker, 1998.

Lee, Lauren K., ed. *The Elementary School Library Collection: A Guide to Books and Other Media.* 19th ed. Willamsport, Pa.: Brodart, 1994.

Price, Anne, and Juliette Yaakov. *Children's Catalog.* 17th ed. New York: H. W. Wilson, 1996.

JEAN CRAIGHEAD GEORGE

Julie of the Wolves

New York: Harper and Row, 1972

Julie, motherless since the age of four, has been raised in two cultures. In one she is Julie Edwards, lives in the village of Mekoryuk, Alaska, and speaks English. In the other she is Miyax and lives at seal camp with Kapugen, her father. Before his disappearance, Kapugen made a pact that his friend's son Daniel would marry Julie when she turned thirteen. Although Julie welcomes the marriage as an escape from her demanding great-aunt, on arriving in Barrow she discovers that Daniel is developmentally delayed and that she is simply another pair of hands to help provide an income for the family. Her friendship with a pen pal from San Francisco becomes a beacon in her unhappy life. When some boys taunt Daniel to attempt marital rape, she runs away.

Although her destination is San Francisco, Julie becomes lost on a barren stretch of Alaska's tundra. To survive, she relies on her father's training, insinuating herself into the nearby pack of wolves by learning to communicate with them. When eventually she does encounter other humans, they lead her to the one person she never expected to see again—her father. As *Booklist* observed, "the well-written, empathetic story effectively evokes the nature of wolves and the traditional Eskimo way of life giving way before the relentless onslaught of civilization."

This book was honored with the 1973 Newbery Medal and continues to engage the hearts and minds of new generations of readers, seeming to confirm *Horn Book*'s 1973 prediction that it is "a book of timeless, perhaps even classic dimensions."

Challenges

Several challenges to the book's presence in schools have been unsuccessful. In June 1982, the Mexico, Missouri, school board ruled against the complainants who tried to have it removed from the district's school libraries because of "socialist, communist, evolutionary, and anti-family themes." In June 1989, the book was retained as required reading in the Littleton, Colorado, elementary schools despite a challenge to move it to the high school reading list because it contained references to family alcoholism, abuse, and divorce; the committee that rejected the complaint concluded that the book showed how the main character overcame her problems and thus modeled good decision-making skills.

Elsewhere it has been removed from elementary reading lists. In 1994, in Chandler, Arizona, its use in a multiage classroom of third, fourth, and fifth grades was challenged by a parent. In 1996 in Pulaski Township, Pennsylvania, it was removed from sixth-grade classes but retained in the district libraries. Other challenges include Palmdale, California (1995), and Ramona, California (1996).

In each of these cases, the rape scene was cited as the reason for the challenge.

Reviews

Booklist 69 (Feb. 1, 1973): 529.

Bulletin of the Center for Children's Books 26 (March 1973): 105.

Christian Science Monitor 66 (Dec. 5, 1973): B12.

Horn Book 49 (Feb. 1973): 54.

Kirkus Reviews 40 (Nov. 15, 1972): 1312.

Library Journal 98 (Jan. 15, 1973): 267.

School Library Journal 31 (Aug. 1985): 28.

Background

Children's Literature Review. Detroit: Gale, 1976. v. 1, pp. 89–94.

Contemporary Authors, New Revision Series. Detroit: Gale, 1989. v. 25, pp. 156–58.

Something about the Author. Detroit: Gale, 1985. v. 68, pp. 78–85.

Sources Recommending This Book

Gillespie, John T. *Best Books for Children Preschool through Grade Six.* 6th ed. New York: R. R. Bowker, 1998.

Homa, Linda L. *The Elementary School Collection.* 22nd ed. Williamsport, Pa.: Brodart, 2000.

Price, Anne, and Juliette Yaakov, eds. *Children's Catalog.* 17th ed. New York: H. W. Wilson, 1996.

Price, Anne, and Juliette Yaakov, eds. *Middle and Junior High School Library Catalog.* 8th ed. New York: H. W. Wilson, 2000.

ROBIE H. HARRIS AND MICHAEL EMBERLEY

It's Perfectly Normal

Cambridge: Candlewick Press, 1994

Straightforward text and explicit illustrations explain the facts of life for young people. The introduction makes clear that the purpose of the book is to address the questions of preadolescent children whose bodies are changing. The author uses the dictionary definitions of the word *sex* to convey its multiple meanings, including gender, sexual reproduction, sexual desire, and sexual intercourse. Each of these is elaborated on in detail, from an explanation and illustration of the male and female reproductive organs to the changes that bodies undergo during puberty to the processes of conception, gestation, and birth.

Emberley's cartoon style enables him to convey information clearly and accurately without a textbook feel; in fact, the illustrations are often humorous, such as the panels that show eggs traveling through the Fallopian tubes into the uterus ("Wheeee!! That was fun!"). Numerous illustrations show naked bodies in various situations and from many angles. Throughout, two cartoon characters, a bird and a bee, comment on the information presented and provide the differing perspectives, as noted in *School Library Journal,* of "early and late bloomers."

Journal of Youth Services in Libraries included *It's Perfectly Normal* in a list of books that belong in a home reference library. Anticipating challenges, Stephanie Zvirin noted in her *Booklist* review that "librarians will find it well worth fighting for if, by some chance, the need arises."

Challenges

Challenged in Provo, Utah, by a library board member who found the book "too racy" for its intended audience and objected to the book's anatomically correct illustrations and discussions of intercourse, masturbation, and homosexuality.

Removed from school district library shelves in Clover Park, Washington.

Unsuccessfully challenged in Charlestown, Pennsylvania, by a group of residents who asked that the book be removed from the children's section at Chester County Public Library, calling it an example of child pornography.

Unsuccessfully challenged in Mexico, Missouri, by a Baptist minister who asked that this book, along with others "concerning family sensitive issues," be removed from the children's section of the public library.

Unsuccessfully challenged at the Fargo, North Dakota, Public Library by those who thought the book was too explicit.

One of several books dealing with sex unsuccessfully challenged at the Placer County Library in Auburn, California.

Reviews

Booklist 91 (Sept. 15, 1994): 133.

Emergency Librarian 23 (March 1996): 43.

Journal of Youth Services 11 (fall 1997): 77.

Kirkus Reviews 62 (Sept. 15, 1994): 1273.

New York Times Book Review 100 (Dec. 3, 1995): 72.

New York Times Book Review 100 (March 12, 1995): 20.

Publishers Weekly 243 (Jan. 29, 1996): 101.

School Library Journal 40 (Dec. 1994): 123.

Wilson Library Bulletin 69 (Dec. 1994): 27.

Background

Sherlin, Kit. "It's Only Normal to Question." *High Plains Reader,* Oct. 11, 1997: 6–7.

Sokolove, Michael. "Sex and the Censors." *Inquirer Magazine* [Philadelphia] (March 9, 1997): 18+.

Zvirin, Stephanie. Interview with Robie Harris. *Booklist* 92 (May 1, 1996): 1495.

Awards and Prizes

ALA Notable Book, 1995

Booklist Editor's Choice, 1994

Boston Globe–Horn Book Honor Book, 1995

New York Times Best Book of the Year, 1995

School Library Journal Best Books, 1994

Wilson Library Bulletin Favorite Reads, 1994

References about the Author

Contemporary Authors. Detroit: Gale, 1997. v. 155, pp. 231–33.

Something about the Author. Detroit: Gale, 1997. v. 90, p. 112–14.

Sources Recommending This Book

Gillespie, John T. *Best Books for Children Preschool through Grade Six.* 6th ed. New York: R. R. Bowker, 1998.

Homa, Linda L., ed. *The Elementary School Library Collection: A Guide to Books and Other Media.* 22nd ed. Willamsport, Pa.: Brodart, 2000.

Price, Anne, and Juliette Yaakov. *Children's Catalog.* 17th ed. New York: H. W. Wilson, 1996.

A Wrinkle in Time

New York: Farrar, Straus and Giroux, 1962

Mr. Murry, who suddenly disappeared while working for the government on a tesseract project, has been gone for a year.* His wife and four children—Meg, Charles Wallace, and the twins, Sandy and Dennys—are extremely worried about his life and whereabouts. Late one stormy night, Meg, Charles Wallace, and their mother are in the kitchen drinking hot chocolate when a strange old lady, Mrs. Whatsit, comes to visit. She warns them that Mr. Murry is in extreme danger and that she and her two friends have come to help save him. Knowing that only they can save their father from the Dark Thing, Meg and Charles Wallace, with the help of their new friend, Calvin O'Keefe, and the three odd women, tesseract through time and space to find Mr. Murry and fight for his life.

Using powerful forces, the group tesseracts to other galaxies and planets in far distant times to accomplish their mission to save Mr. Murry. Throughout this harrowing journey, the traveling companions encounter many dreadful creatures and experience many frightening situations. Although Charles Wallace and Calvin are brave, Meg, in an act of courage and love, endangers her own life by tesseracting back to the place where Charles Wallace has accidentally been left behind. She saves Charles Wallace, proving that love does triumph over evil.

Published in 1962, this novel was one of the first to portray women as positive role models for young readers. Mrs. Murry is a scientist, certainly not a typical career for a mother in the 1960s, and the main protagonist, Meg, is the true heroine in this powerful novel of the desperate struggle between good and evil. Meg is one of just a few female main characters in science fiction books for children that were being published at the time. Over the past decades, these two female characters have remained strong role models for young girls throughout the country.

Using tidbits of information from the disciplines of religion, science, and philosophy and combining them with satire and allegory, L'Engle has written a sometimes confusing but dramatic and compelling science fiction novel. This winner of the 1963 Newbery Medal remains popular fare for sci-fi fans.

Challenges

Challenged, but retained, by the Catawba County School Board in Newton, North Carolina (1996). A parent requested the book be pulled from the school libraries because it allegedly undermines religious beliefs.

---

* Tesseract (verb): To travel the shortest distance between two points, not by moving in a straight line but by a fold or wrinkle.

Because the book sends a mixed signal to children about good and evil, the book was challenged in the Anniston, Alabama, schools in 1990. The complainant also objected to listing the name of Jesus Christ together with the names of great artists, philosophers, scientists, and religious leaders when referring to defenders of Earth against evil.

Challenged, but retained, on the media-center shelves of the Polk City, Florida, Elementary School in 1985.

Reviews

Booklist 58 (April 1, 1962): 535.

Horn Book 38 (April 1962): 177.

Library Journal 87 (March 15, 1962): 1332.

Wilson Library Bulletin 58 (May 1962): 182.

Background

Dohner, Jan. "Literature of Change: Science Fiction and Women." *Top of the News* (spring 1978): 261–65.

Gonzales, Doreen. *Madeleine L'Engle: Author of* A Wrinkle in Time. New York: Dillon Press, 1991.

Jones, Raymond E. *A Literature Guide to* A Wrinkle in Time. Cambridge, Mass.: Book Wise, 1991.

Rakow, Susan R. "Young-Adult Literature for Honors Students?" *English Journal* 80 (Jan. 1991): 48–51.

Awards and Prizes

Hans Christian Andersen Award runner-up, 1964

Lewis Carroll Shelf Award, 1965

Newbery Medal, 1963

Sequoyah Children's Book Award, from the Oklahoma State Department of Education, 1965

References about the Author

Children's Literature Review. Detroit: Gale, 1988. v. 14, pp. 132–56; v. 1, pp. 129–34.

Contemporary Authors. Detroit: Gale, 1967. v. 1–4, pp. 582–83.

Contemporary Authors, New Revision Series. Detroit: Gale, 1992. v. 39, pp. 226–30; v. 21, pp. 240–43; v. 3, pp. 331–32.

Contemporary Literary Criticism. Detroit: Gale, 1980. v. 12, pp. 346–52.

Dictionary of Literary Biography. Detroit: Gale, 1986. v. 52, pp. 241–49.

Something about the Author. Detroit: Gale, 1994. v. 75, pp. 114–21; v. 27, pp. 131–40; v. 1, pp. 141–42.

Sources Recommending This Book

"Becoming a Lifetime Reader." *Book Links* 87 (Jan. 15, 1991): 1018–21.

Children's Catalog. 16th ed. Ed. Juliette Yaakov. New York: H. W. Wilson, 1991.

Eaken, Mary K., comp. *Good Books for Children: A Selection of Outstanding Children's Books Published 1950–1965.* Chicago: University of Chicago Press, 1966.

Estes, Sally, ed. *Growing Up Is Hard to Do.* Chicago: American Library Association, 1994.

Freeman, Judy. *Books Kids Will Sit Still For: The Complete Read-Aloud Guide.* 2nd ed. New York: R. R. Bowker, 1990.

Gillespie, John T., ed. *Best Books for Junior High Readers.* New Providence, N.J.: R. R. Bowker, 1991.

Gillespie, John T. *The Elementary School Paperback Collection.* Chicago: American Library Association, 1985.

Gillespie, John T. *The Junior High School Paperback Collection.* Chicago: American Library Association, 1985.

Gillespie, John T., and Christine Gilbert, eds. *Best Books for Children: Preschool through the Middle Grades.* 3rd ed. New York: R. R. Bowker, 1985.

Junior High School Library Catalog. 16th ed. Ed. Juliette Yaakov. New York: H. W. Wilson, 1990.

Lee, Lauren K., ed. *The Elementary School Library Collection: A Guide to Books and Other Media.* 18th ed. Williamsport, Pa.: Brodart, 1992.

Middle and Junior High School Library Catalog. 7th ed. Ed. Anne Price and Juliette Yaakov. New York: H. W. Wilson, 1995.

Miller, Frances A. "Books to Read When You Hate to Read." *Booklist* 88 (Feb. 15, 1992): 1101.

Mockett, Sara, and Ann Weltori. "Fiction for the Gifted." *Booklist* 88 (Sept. 1, 1991): 66–67.

"See How They Grow." *Children's Literature in Education* 18 (spring 1987): 37.

"Still Good Reading: Adolescent Novels Written before 1967." *English Journal* 81 (April 1992): 90.

The Giver

New York: Houghton Mifflin, 1993

This Newbery Medal–winning book, written by acclaimed children's author Lois Lowry, tells the story of Jonas as he reaches his twelfth year—when he will become a Twelve and receive his life assignment. Jonas and his family—his parents and his sister, Lily, who is a Six—live in a community that has adopted Sameness. In this futuristic community, individuals are spared from making any decisions; instead, a group of Elders make all decisions for the good of the group.

Jonas's protected life is shattered when he learns that his life assignment is to be that of Receiver of Memory—the one person in the community who maintains memories of the time before Sameness. When Jonas begins his training with the former Receiver, who is now known as the Giver, he receives pleasant memories—sunsets, sailing, holidays, sunshine, and color—that existed before Sameness. Eventually, he is forced to experience unpleasant emotions—sadness, loneliness, and pain. Jonas is forbidden from discussing what he has learned with other members of the community, who remain protected from emotions and pain. Jonas's isolation grows as he begins to experience what his family and friends will never understand—music, love, colors.

Jonas is forced to make a decision when he learns that Gabriel—a baby whom the family has been caring for—is to be "released" for failing to thrive. Before becoming the Receiver, Jonas thought that being released merely meant going to another place—the mythical Elsewhere—but he learns that release actually means death. To make matters worse, Jonas's father, who is a Nurturer, is assigned to do the release. With the blessings of the Giver, Jonas takes the baby and sets off on his bike in search of Elsewhere.

The Giver presents complicated issues—euthanasia, conformity, and the suppression of personal liberty, among others. By identifying with Jonas, however, readers are clearly aware of the problems of this society. Lowry may not provide readers with a happy ending, but neither does she give us the answers.

Horn Book wrote, "The story is skillfully written; the air of disquiet is delicately insinuated. And the theme of balancing the values of freedom and security is beautifully presented."

Challenges

Challenged, but retained, at a Lake Butler, Florida, public middle school (1999). A parent complained because the issues of infanticide and sexual awakening are discussed in the book.

Challenged at the Troy Intermediate School in Avon Lake, Ohio (1999), as an "optional" reading choice for sixth-grade students. A pastor objected to the book's "mature themes"—suicide, sexuality, and euthanasia.

Challenged at the Lakota High School in Cincinnati, Ohio (1996).

Restricted to students with parental permission in the Columbia Falls, Montana, school system (1995) because of the book's treatment of themes of infanticide and euthanasia.

Temporarily banned from classes by the Bonita Unified School District in La Verne and San Dimas, California (1994), after four parents complained that violent and sexual passages were inappropriate for children.

Reviews

Booklist 89 (April 15, 1993): 1506.

Bulletin of the Center for Children's Books 46 (April 1993): 257.

Horn Book 69 (July 1993): 458.

Publishers Weekly 240 (Feb. 15, 1993): 240.

School Library Journal 39 (May 1993): 124.

Voice of Youth Advocates 16 (Aug. 1993): 167.

Wilson Library Bulletin 68 (Oct. 1993): 122.

Articles about This Book

Campbell, Patty. "The Sand in the Oyster." *Horn Book* 69 (Nov./Dec. 1993): 717–21.

"The Gift of Memory." (using Lois Lowry's *The Giver* with grades 7–12) *School Librarian's Workshop* 14 (April 1994): 8–9.

Lowry, Lois. "1994 Newbery Acceptance Speech." *Journal of Youth Services in Libraries* 7 (summer 1994): 361–67.

Silvey, Anita. "The Giver." (Lois Lowry's new book and risk taking in children's literature) *Horn Book* 69 (July/Aug. 1993): 392.

Walters, Karla. "Other Voices: Pills against Sexual 'Stirrings' in Lowry's The Giver." *Bookbird* 32 (summer 1994): 35–36.

Background

Haley-James, Shirley. "Lois Lowry." *Horn Book* 66 (July/Aug. 1990): 422–24.

Lorraine, Walter. "Lois Lowry." *Horn Book* 70 (July/Aug. 1994): 423–26.

Smith, Amanda. "PW Interviews: Lois Lowry." (writer of young adults' books) *Publishers Weekly* 229 (Feb. 21, 1986): 152–53.

Woolf, Vera, Patricia Conover, and Alice Resnick. "Focus On: Lois Lowry." (discussion and writing activities) *School Librarian's Workshop* 12 (April 1992): 6–7.

Awards and Prizes

Newbery Medal, 1994

Anastasia Krupnik

Boston: Houghton Mifflin, 1979

Anastasia at Your Service

Boston: Houghton Mifflin, 1982

Anastasia Krupnik and *Anastasia at Your Service* are the first and third of a nine-book series featuring Anastasia, a character that *Horn Book* has called "one of the most intriguing female protagonists to appear in children's books since the advent of Harriet the spy." Reviewers consistently remark on Lowry's ability to fuse the comic and the serious in these books.

Anastasia is ten and on the brink of numerous changes when readers first meet her in *Anastasia Krupnik*. Her need for certainty in life plays itself out in the lists she creates: "Things I Love" and "Things I Hate." But these very lists demonstrate the ambiguity of life, as so many of the elements—her teacher, for one—migrate back and forth between columns. The least ambiguous parts of her life are also the hardest for her to accept: her imminent new sibling and the decline of the grandmother who no longer even recognizes her. According to *Booklist*, "Humor filters through the dialogue as superbly developed characters react to the vicissitudes of life; and through them Lowry creates situations that can give a reader insight."

In *Anastasia at Your Service,* Anastasia is twelve. She has adjusted well to big-sisterhood and to her family's move from Cambridge to a Boston suburb, although she hasn't been there long enough to make many friends. At loose ends when summer begins, she decides to find work and, inspired by old novels, advertises herself as a "lady's companion." The job she lands turns out to be more a maid than companion, and her employer, she discovers, is the grandmother of a classmate. For this book, *Booklist* found Lowry "right on target in capturing the thoughts and emotions of a twelve-year-old girl." *Horn Book* praised Lowry's "lively picture of a happy, devoted family. Anastasia is the fortunate possessor of two of the most sensible, sympathetic, cheerful, and amusing parents in children's literature, and her little brother Sam is a delight."

Other books in this series include *Anastasia Again!* (1981), *Anastasia, Ask Your Analyst* (1984), *Anastasia on Her Own* (1985), *Anastasia Has the Answers* (1986), *Anastasia's Chosen Career* (1987), *Anastasia at This Address* (1991), and *Anastasia, Absolutely* (1995).

Challenges

Anastasia Krupnik

Removed from the library shelves in one elementary school in Cayce–West Columbia, South Carolina, School District in

1999 for "use of a vulgarity for human waste." Case resulted in school board's revision of selection policy to include appropriateness of language in buying decisions.

Removed from the Stevens Point, Wisconsin, School District's elementary recommended reading list in 1993 because of profanity and references to underage drinking; decision reversed later in year under condition that parents be given recommended reading lists containing descriptive paragraphs on the book's contents.

Unsuccessful challenge in 1992 to remove book from school libraries in Wichita, Kansas, for being offensive.

Removed from the Roosevelt Elementary School library, Tulare, California, in 1986 by the school principal because of a parent complaint over language (the phrase "crock of shit" appears twice in the book); book returned to shelves with the word "shit" whited out in both places.

Anastasia at Your Service

One of sixteen books by Judy Blume and Lois Lowry in school library collections in Casper, Wyoming, challenged by a couple who accused the books of being "subtle and filthy" and instruments that "sexually and socially pervert, abuse, and scandalize innocent children."

Reviews

Anastasia Krupnik

Booklist 76 (Oct. 15, 1979): 354.

Bulletin of the Center for Children's Books 33 (Jan. 1980): 99.

Children's Book Review Service 8 (Jan. 1980): 47.

Horn Book 55 (Dec. 1979): 663.

Reading Teacher 34 (Oct. 1980): 103.

Anastasia at Your Service

Booklist 79 (Sept. 1, 1982): 46.

Bulletin of the Center for Children's Books 36 (Dec. 1982): 72.

Horn Book 58 (Dec. 1982): 650.

Language Arts 60 (March 1983): 360.

Los Angeles Times Book Review (Aug. 5, 1984): 4.

Publishers Weekly 222 (Nov. 12, 1982): 67.

School Library Journal 29 (Nov. 1982): 47.

Background

Kimmel, Eric A. "Anastasia Agonistes: The Tragicomedy of Lois Lowry." *Horn Book* 63 (March/April 1987): 181–87.

Smith, Amanda. "PW Interviews: Lois Lowry." *Publishers Weekly* 229 (Feb. 21, 1986): 152–53.

Awards and Prizes

Lowry: Twice winner of the Newbery Medal, in 1990 for *Number the Stars* (Houghton Mifflin, 1989) and in 1994 for *The Giver* (Houghton Mifflin, 1993)

References about the Author

Children's Literature Review. Detroit: Gale, 1984. v. 6, pp. 192–96.

Contemporary Authors, New Revision Series. Detroit: Gale, 1984. v. 13, pp. 333–36.

Contemporary Authors, New Revision Series. Detroit: Gale, 1994. v. 43, pp. 280–82.

Something about the Author. Detroit: Gale, 1993. v. 70, pp. 134–37.

Something about the Author Autobiography Series. Detroit: Gale, 1986. v. 3, pp. 131–46.

Sources Recommending Books in This Series

Gillespie, John T. *Best Books for Children Preschool through Grade Six*. 6th ed. New York: R. R. Bowker, 1998.

Lee, Lauren K., ed. *The Elementary School Library Collection: A Guide to Books and Other Media*. 19th ed. Willamsport, Pa.: Brodart, 1994.

Price, Anne, and Juliette Yaakov. *Children's Catalog*. 17th ed. New York: H. W. Wilson, 1996.

The Agony of Alice
New York: Atheneum, 1985

Alice in Rapture, Sort Of
New York: Atheneum, 1989

Reluctantly Alice
New York: Atheneum, 1991

All But Alice
New York: Atheneum, 1992

Alice in April
New York: Atheneum, 1993

Alice In-Between
New York: Atheneum, 1994

Alice the Brave
New York: Atheneum, 1995

Alice in Lace
New York: Atheneum, 1996

Outrageously Alice
New York: Atheneum, 1997

Achingly Alice
New York: Atheneum, 1998

Alice on the Outside
New York: Atheneum, 1999

The Grooming of Alice
New York: Atheneum, 2000

Alice Alone
New York: Atheneum, 2001

The thirteen books published in this series to date trace Alice McKinley's growth from the summer before sixth grade, when she is a newcomer to Silver Spring, Maryland, to the fall of ninth grade. Each book is episodic in nature and reflects natural occurrences in Alice's growing-up process, from the time she gets her first period (*The Agony of Alice*) and first boyfriend (*Alice in Rapture, Sort Of*) to her angst at being ordinary (*Outrageously Alice*) and her growing understanding of life's complexities (*Achingly Alice*).

Because her mother died when Alice was four, she must rely on her father and her brother, Lester, seven years her senior, for guidance in everyday matters. For the female perspective, Alice often turns to her Aunt Sally in Chicago and later to Crystal, one of her brother's several girl-friends.

Like all children, Alice and her friends are curious about all sorts of things, including matters of the body. In *Reluctantly Alice*, motherless Alice sees breasts for the first time in seventh-grade P.E.

class, and when her friend Elizabeth wonders what a naked male looks like, Alice helps her find pictures in anatomy books at the library, where she learns that "it's okay to be curious." Frances Bradburn of *Wilson Library Journal* wrote that "*Reluctantly Alice* isn't just about junior high obsession with bodies, boys, and sex; it is about growing up, coping, and becoming an effective person through all stages of development."

In other books, Alice agonizes about an appointment with a male doctor; conquers her fear of water and learns to swim; puzzles over unfamiliar terms she and her friends encounter in *Arabian Nights,* which Elizabeth has "borrowed" from her mother's bedroom; participates in a wedding and the lingerie shower that precedes it; addresses issues regarding pregnancy, marriage, car ownership, and more in her eighth-grade Critical Choices class; and experiences her first heartbreak.

Critics have called books in this series "a novelized handbook on adolescence" (*Horn Book*) and "a road map for a girl coming of age today, not in any direct self-help way but as a candid view of how hard it is to follow the unwritten rules" (*Booklist*). Alice is eleven in the first book and fourteen in the most recent. Naylor, who won the 1992 Newbery Medal for *Shiloh,* plans to continue the series until Alice is eighteen. Age ranges suggested by publishers and reviewers begin at 8–12 and move up according to Alice's age in the book, which seems to determine the top of the range. In a review of *Outrageously Alice,* the *Horn Book* has suggested that the books are most suitable for the "older middle-school readers who have themselves been growing up along with Alice." The trim size is smaller for *Alice on the Outside,* giving this and subsequent titles a young-adult look.

Challenges

Series

Removed from sixth-grade required reading list in Monroe, Connecticut, after challenge by parents, who objected to the sexual content of the books. Although the series was defended by the director of the Monroe Public Library, the challenge was upheld by the superintendent of schools.

The Agony of Alice

Challenged in Fairfax County, Virginia, by the parents of a fifth-grader in McLean, Virginia, who wanted it removed from the school after their daughter read it for a school assignment. Three chapters of the book are contained in an anthology sometimes used in the Fairfax County schools. The school and district review committee recommended that the book be kept in the library and the anthology remain available for classroom instruction, and the school superintendent urged school librarians not to deny access to the book.

All But Alice

The parents of an eight-year-old in Rosemount, Minnesota, who checked the book out of the school library, objected to passages in which Alice and her brother discuss song lyrics dealing with sexual activities, including necrophilia. They asked that the book be removed from all the elementary school libraries in the district; the challenge was unsuccessful. In Thorndike, Maine, the parent of a fourth-grader who checked the book out of the school library objected to passages in the book; the school board decided to retain the book but restrict it to students in fifth grade or higher with parental permission required.

Reviews

The Agony of Alice

Booklist 87 (Feb. 15, 1991): 1217.

Booklist 87 (Nov. 1, 1990): 535.

Booklist 88 (May 1, 1992): 1612.

Reading Teacher 40 (March 1987): 617.

Reading Teacher 40 (Oct. 1986): 52.

Washington Post Book World 19 (Nov. 5, 1989): 27.

Alice in Rapture, Sort Of

Booklist 86 (April 15, 1990): 1635.

Emergency Librarian 17 (Sept. 1989): 48.

Language Arts 66 (Dec. 1989): 886.

Publishers Weekly 238 (July 12, 1991): 67.

School Library Journal 42 (May 1996): 50.

Reluctantly Alice

Booklist 87 (Feb. 1, 1991): 1127.

Bulletin of the Center for Children's Books 44 (April 1991): 201.

Emergency Librarian (Sept./Oct. 1991): 49.

Horn Book 67 (July 1991): 458.

Kirkus Reviews 59 (Feb. 1, 1991): 176.

Kliatt Young Adult Paperback Book Guide 27 (Jan. 1993): 10.

Library Talk 4 (Sept. 1991): 27.

Publishers Weekly 238 (April 12, 1991): 58.

Publishers Weekly 239 (Oct. 5, 1992): 73.

School Library Journal 37 (March 1991): 193.

School Library Journal 42 (May 1996): 50.

Voice of Youth Advocates 14 (June 1991): 100.

Wilson Library Bulletin (June 1991): 109.

All But Alice

Booklist 88 (March 1, 1992): 1272.

Bulletin of the Center for Children's Books 45 (May 1992): 244.

Children's Bookwatch 4 (July 1994): 7.

Five Owls 6 (May 1992): 69.

Horn Book 68 (July 1992): 453.

Kirkus Reviews 60 (Apr. 1, 1992): 470.

Kliatt Young Adult Paperback Book Guide 28 (Sept. 1994): 10.

Library Talk 6 (Jan. 1993): 51.

Reading Teacher 47 (Oct. 1993): 138.

School Library Journal 38 (May 1992): 116.

Voice of Youth Advocates 15 (June 1992): 98.

Alice in April

Booklist 89 (March 1, 1993): 1223.

Bulletin of the Center for Children's Books 46 (March 1993): 222.

Journal of Reading 37 (Nov. 1993): 248.

Kirkus Reviews 61 (March 1, 1993): 303.

Reading Teacher 48 (Oct. 1994): 156.

School Library Journal 39 (June 1993): 109.

Voice of Youth Advocates 16 (June 1993): 92.

Alice In-Between

Book Report 13 (Sept. 1994): 41.

Booklist 90 (May 1, 1994): 1601.

Bulletin of the Center for Children's Books 47 (May 1994): 296.

Children's Bookwatch 6 (July 1996): 5.

English Journal 84 (Sept. 1995): 117.

Horn Book 70 (July 1994): 479.

New Advocate 8 (winter 1995): 59.

School Library Journal 40 (June 1994): 133.

Voice of Youth Advocates 17 (Aug. 1994): 148.

Alice the Brave

Booklist 91 (May 1, 1995): 1575.

Bulletin of the Center for Children's Books 48 (April 1995): 283.

Horn Book 71 (July 1995): 485.

Journal of Adolescent and Adult Literacy 39 (Oct. 1995): 169.

Kirkus Reviews 63 (April 1, 1995): 473.

Parents' Choice 19 (Nov. 1995): 11.

School Library Journal 41 (May 1995): 121.

Voice of Youth Advocates 18 (Oct. 1995): 221.

Alice in Lace

Booklist 92 (March 1, 1996): 1174.

Bulletin of the Center for Children's Books 49 (April 1996): 273.

Horn Book 72 (May 1996): 357.

Kirkus Reviews 64 (Feb. 15, 1996): 298.

Publishers Weekly 243 (March 4, 1996): 67.

School Library Journal 42 (April 1996): 138.

Voice of Youth Advocates 19 (Aug. 1996): 159.

Outrageously Alice

Booklist 93 (May 15, 1997): 1573.

Bulletin of the Center for Children's Books 50 (July 1997): 405.

Horn Book 73 (July 1997): 460.

Journal of Adolescent and Adult Literacy 41 (Feb. 1998): 409.

Kirkus Reviews 65 (April 15, 1997): 645.

New York Times Book Review 102 (July 6, 1997): 16.

Publishers Weekly 244 (April 21, 1997): 73.

School Library Journal 43 (June 1997): 122.

Voice of Youth Advocates 20 (Oct. 1997): 246.

Achingly Alice

Booklist 94 (April 1, 1998): 1312.

Bulletin of the Center for Children's Books 51 (April 1998): 290.

Horn Book 74 (May/June 1998): 348.

School Library Journal 44 (June 1998): 148.

Alice on the Outside

Booklist 95 (May 1, 1999): 1586.

Bulletin of the Center for Children's Books 52 (June 1999): 359.

Horn Book 75 (July/Aug. 1999): 471–72.

School Library Journal 45 (July 1999): 99.

The Grooming of Alice

Horn Book 76 (July/Aug. 2000): 463.

Kliatt 34 (July 2000): 11.

School Library Journal 46 (May 2000): 175.

Voice of Youth Advocates 23 (Oct. 2000): 269.

Alice Alone

Horn Book 77 (July/Aug. 2001): 459.

Kliatt 35 (May 2001): 13.

Background

Naylor, Phyllis. "Censored." *Parenting* (Feb. 1995): 106–7.

Naylor, Phyllis. Excerpts from letter to a teacher who objected to *Shiloh*. *Censorship Matters* 3 (1994).

Naylor, Phyllis. *How I Came to Be a Writer,* rev. ed. New York: Aladdin, 1987.

Naylor, Phyllis. Newbery Acceptance Speech. *Horn Book* (July 1992): 404–9.

Naylor, Rex. "Phyllis Reynolds Naylor." *Horn Book* (July 1992): 412–15.

Official Alice website. Includes readers' questions, answered by Naylor. http://www.simonsayskids.com/alice

Awards and Prizes

Alice in April: ALA Reluctant Young Adult Readers, 1994

Outrageously Alice: ALA Best Books for Young Adults, 1998; VOYA Best Books for Young Adults, 1998

Reluctantly Alice: School Library Journal Best Books of 1991

References about the Author

Children's Literature Review. Detroit: Gale, 1989. v. 17, pp. 48–62.

Contemporary Authors, New Revision Series. Detroit: Gale, 1988. v. 24, pp. 334–35.

Contemporary Authors, New Revision Series. Detroit: Gale, 1998. v. 59, pp. 284–88.

Something about the Author. Detroit: Gale, 1999. v. 102, pp. 149–56.

Sources Recommending Books in This Series

Best Books for Children Preschool through Grade Six. New York: R. R. Bowker. Various editions.

The Elementary School Library Collection: A Guide to Books and Other Media. Willamsport, Pa.: Brodart. Various editions.

Price, Anne, and Juliette Yaakov. *Children's Catalog.* 17th ed. New York: H. W. Wilson, 1996.

LESLEA NEWMAN

Heather Has Two Mommies

Northhampton, Mass.: In Other Words, 1989

This picture book tells the story of Heather, the daughter of a lesbian couple. The reader discovers how Heather's parents met and decided to have a baby, and the story proceeds through Heather's early childhood to her enrollment in a preschool. At this point, through her interactions with the other children, Heather learns her family is different because she does not have a father. The teacher asks the children to draw pictures of their families, revealing that each child has a different configuration of family members.

Heather Has Two Mommies is an exploration of the nature of families in general, while focusing on lesbian parents in particular.

The book is most successful when dealing with the question of family structure. It is interesting to see the preschool teacher illustrate to the children that every family is different in some way by having the children draw their family portraits. There is great warmth in this part of the book, and it is easy to see why Heather is comforted after the teacher hangs the pictures in the classroom. The book is least successful when discussing the mechanics of Heather's conception. The book, written for an audience of early-elementary-age children, presupposes that its readers have a working knowledge of the reproductive process. Such concepts as "sperm and egg" and terms like "vagina" are used to describe to young readers the process of artificial insemination. All of this is clearly beyond the comprehension of most readers in the book's target audience.

Nevertheless, *Heather Has Two Mommies* provides validation of children in different family situations. For children of other kinds of families, the book shows that each family is special, which is important in a day when the family consisting of a mother, father, son, and daughter is no longer the norm.

Challenges

Challenged, but retained, in the juvenile nonfiction section of the Nampa, Idaho, Public Library (1999).

Challenged at the Wichita Falls, Texas, Public Library (1998). The deacon body of the First Baptist Church requested that any literature that promotes or sanctions a homosexual lifestyle be removed. The Wichita Falls City Council established a policy that allows library card holders who collect three hundred signatures to have children's books moved to an adult section of the library. U.S. District Court Judge Jerry Buchmeyer struck down the library resolution as unconstitutional and the books were returned.

Challenged at the Chandler, Arizona, Public Library (1994) because the book is a "skillful presentation to the young child about lesbianism/homosexuality."

Removed by officials at the Lane County Head Start Center in Cottage Grove, Oregon, in 1994.

Challenged, but retained, in the Oak Bluffs, Massachusetts, School Library in 1994. Though the parent leading the protest stated, "The subject matter . . . is obscene and vulgar and the message is that homosexuality is okay," the selection review committee voted unanimously to keep the book.

Challenged, but retained, at the Dayton and Montgomery County, Ohio, Public Library in 1993.

Challenged at the Mesa, Arizona, Public Library (1993) because it "is vile, sick, and goes against every law and constitution."

Challenged at the North Brunswick, New Jersey, Public Library in 1993.

Challenged at the Cumberland County, North Carolina, Public Library in 1993.

Challenged at the Wicomico County Free Library in Salisbury, Maryland, in 1993.

Moved from the children's section to the adult section at the Mercer County Library System, in Lawrence, New Jersey, in 1993.

Moved from the children's section to the adult section in an Elizabethtown, North Carolina, library (1993) because it "promotes a dangerous and ungodly lifestyle from which children must be protected."

Moved from the children's section to the young adult section at the Chestatee Regional Library System in Gainesville, Georgia, in 1993. Three area legislators wanted the book removed and said, "We could put together a resolution to amend the Georgia state constitution to say that tax dollars cannot be used to promote homosexuality, pedophilia, or sado-masochism."

Because the school board objected to words that were "age inappropriate," the book was removed from the Brooklyn, New York, School District's curriculum in 1992.

Challenged in Fayetteville, North Carolina, in 1992.

Reviews

Booklist 86 (March 1, 1990): 1354.

Bulletin of the Center for Children's Books 43 (Feb. 1990): 144.

Small Press Book Review 6 (July 1990): 20.

Articles about This Book

Loch, Marge Wouters. "Children's Cornucopia: Whose Family's Values? Gay and Lesbian Families in Children's Books." *WLW Journal* 15 (winter 1992/1993): 13–14.

Background

Ford, Michael Thomas. "Gay Books for Young Readers: When Caution Calls the Shots." *Publishers Weekly* 241 (Feb. 21, 1994): 24–27.

References about the Author

Contemporary Authors. Detroit: Gale, 1989. v. 126, pp. 321–22.

Something about the Author. Detroit: Gale, 1993. v. 71, pp. 138–39.

Bridge to Terabithia

New York: HarperCollins, 1977

Jess Aarons is determined to become the best runner in his school; he's so determined that he practices daily over the summer in preparation. To his amazement, he is easily beaten in a race on the first day of school by a newcomer to the school and his new neighbor, Leslie Burke.

Although at first Jess is irritated with Leslie, eventually they become friends. Jess comes to appreciate the world Leslie comes from—a world he doesn't know that includes music, art, and culture—and Leslie uses her incredible imagination to create a secret kingdom in the woods, where the two of them rule, called Terabithia.

Their peaceful world is shattered one day when Jess is on a trip to Washington, D.C., and Leslie attempts to cross the rain-swollen river to Terabithia alone. The rope breaks, and Leslie hits her head on a stone as she falls. After Leslie's death, Jess deals with the emotional impact of the tragedy. At the end of the story, Jess builds a bridge to Terabithia and takes his sister there safely.

In this Newbery Medal–winning book, Paterson weaves a tale of friendship and tragedy. Jack Forman, reviewing for *School Library Journal,* wrote, "Jess and Leslie are so effectively developed as characters that young readers might well feel that they were their classmates." The reviewer in the *Bulletin of the Center for Children's Books* writes, "Quite unlike Paterson's previous books in setting or theme, this is just as beautifully crafted and convincing, but even more touching."

Public Media Video produced a movie based on the book as part of their Wonderworks series. The movie won an American Film and Video Festival Blue Ribbon in 1992.

Challenges

Removed from the fifth-grade classrooms of the New Brighton Area School District in Pulaski Township, Pennsylvania (1996), because of "profanity, disrespect of adults, and an elaborate fantasy world they felt might lead to confusion."

In 1995, a group of parents asked the Medway, Maine, school board to stop fifth-grade students from reading two books in class. The parents charged that *The Castle in the Attic,* by Elizabeth Winthrop, and *Bridge to Terabithia* use swear words and deal with sorcery.

Challenged in the Gettysburg, Pennsylvania, public schools (1993) because of offensive language.

In 1993, a challenge to this book in Oskaloosa, Kansas, led to the enactment of a new policy mandating that teachers examine their required material for profanities. Teachers will list each profanity and the number of times it is used in the book and forward the list to parents, who will be asked to give written permission for their children to read the material.

Challenged at the Mechanicsburg, Pennsylvania, Area School District (1992) because of profanity and reference to witchcraft.

Challenged as suitable curriculum material in the Harwinton and Burlington, Connecticut, schools (1986) because it contains language and subject matter that set bad examples and give students negative views of life.

Challenged as sixth-grade recommended reading in the Lincoln, Nebraska, schools (1986) because it contains "profanity," including the phrase "Oh, Lord" and "Lord" used as an expletive.

Reviews

Booklist 74 (Nov. 15, 1977): 554.

Bulletin of the Center for Children's Books 31 (Dec. 1977): 66.

Horn Book 54 (Feb. 1978): 48.

School Librarian 27 (June 1979): 165.

School Library Journal 24 (Nov. 1977): 61.

Articles about This Book

Gage, Marilyn Kay. "Katherine Paterson." (projects for nine of her books) *School Library Media Activities Monthly* 8 (Nov. 1991): 26–29.

Hass, Elizabeth, and Patricia Light. "Reading about Death." *Parents* 60 (Aug. 1985): 74–75.

Awards and Prizes

Lewis Carroll Shelf Award, 1978

Michigan Young Reader's Award, Division Two runner-up, 1980

Newbery Medal, 1978

Notable Children's Book, 1977

School Library Journal's Best Books of the Year, 1977

References about the Author

Children's Literature Review. Detroit: Gale, 1984. v. 7, pp. 224–43.

Contemporary Authors. Detroit: Gale, 1977. v. 21–24, p. 662.

Contemporary Authors, New Revision Series. Detroit: Gale, 1990. v. 28, pp. 359–64.

Contemporary Literary Criticism. Detroit: Gale, 1980. v. 30, pp. 282–87; v. 12, p. 485.

Dictionary of Literary Biography. Detroit: Gale, 1986. v. 52, pp. 296–314.

Something about the Author. Detroit: Gale, 1988. v. 53, pp. 118–28; v. 13, 176–77.

Sources Recommending This Book

Children's Catalog. 16th ed. Ed. Juliette Yaakov. New York: H. W. Wilson, 1991.

Colborn, Candy. *What Do Children Read Next? A Reader's Guide to Fiction for Children.* Detroit: Gale, 1994.

Donavin, Denise Perry. *Best of the Best for Children.* Chicago: American Library Association, 1992.

Estes, Sally, ed. *Growing Up Is Hard to Do.* Chicago: American Library Association, 1994.

Freeman, Judy. *Books Kids Will Sit Still For: The Complete Read-Aloud Guide.* 2nd ed. New York: R. R. Bowker, 1990.

Gillespie, John T. *The Elementary School Paperback Collection.* Chicago: American Library Association, 1985.

Gillespie, John T. *The Junior High School Paperback Collection*. Chicago: American Library Assocation, 1985.

Gillespie, John T., and Christine Gilbert, eds. *Best Books for Children: Preschool through the Middle Grades*. 3rd ed. New York: R. R. Bowker, 1985.

Junior High School Library Catalog. 16th ed. Ed. Juliette Yaakov. New York: H. W. Wilson, 1990.

Lee, Lauren K., ed. *The Elementary School Library Collection: A Guide to Books and Other Media*. 18th ed. Williamsport, Pa.: Brodart, 1992.

Middle and Junior High School Library Catalog. 7th ed. Ed. Anne Price and Juliette Yaakov. New York: H. W. Wilson, 1995.

Rochman, Hazel. *Against Borders: Promoting Books for a Multicultural World*. Chicago: American Library Association, 1993.

Rudman, Marsha Kabakow, Kathleen Dunne Gagne, and Joanne E. Berstein. *Books to Help Children Cope with Separation and Loss: An Annotated Bibliography*. 4th ed. New Providence, N.J.: R. R. Bowker, 1993.

The Young Adult Reader's Adviser: The Best in Social Sciences, History, Science and Health. Vol. 2. Ed. Myra Immell. New Providence, N.J.: R. R. Bowker, 1992.

The Great Gilly Hopkins

New York: T. Y. Crowell, 1978

Abandoned long ago by her California-bound flower-child mother, Gilly Hopkins is intelligent, cool, and scheming, and has been bounced from one foster home to the next. Placed in Maime Trotter's residence for what she hopes will be a short stay, Gilly finds her new foster home unappealing and begins stealing from Mr. Randolph, a blind neighbor. Gilly also undertakes a letter-writing campaign to her mother. This unexpectedly results in the appearance of her previously unknown grandmother, with whom Gilly eventually goes to live.

During her time at Maime Trotter's, Gilly expects to continue with her usual behavior, but something changes. Gilly's experiences with Maime; William Ernest, another child in Maime's house; and Mr. Randolph teach her what it means to care for others. She eventually realizes that the large, untidy Trotter house is actually a house full of wisdom and love.

Booklist wrote that "this perceptive story draws strength from its finely delineated characters and rich, moving narrative."

The book was adapted for television.

Challenges

Challenged because of explicit language, but retained in the Lander County, Nevada, School District (1997).

Challenged at the Walnut Elementary School in Emporia, Kansas (1993), by parents who said that it contained profanity and graphic violence.

Challenged at the Alamo Heights, Texas, School District elementary schools (1992) because it contains the words "hell" and "damn."

Pulled from, but later restored to, the language arts curriculum at four Cheshire, Connecticut, elementary schools (1991) because the book is "filled with profanity, blasphemy and obscenities, and gutter language."

Reviews

Booklist 74 (March 15, 1978): 1194.

Bulletin of the Center for Children's Books 31 (May 1978): 146.

Catholic Library World 50 (Nov. 1978): 180.

Horn Book 54 (June 1978): 279.

Publishers Weekly 213 (Feb. 13, 1978): 127.

Publishers Weekly 215 (June 18, 1979): 94.

Publishers Weekly 224 (Dec. 2, 1983): 89.

School Librarian 27 (Dec. 1979): 383.

School Library Journal 24 (April 1978): 87.

Articles about This Book

Elleman, Barbara. *"Learning's* Summer Reading for Children." *Learning* 12 (April/May 1984): 72.

Sharp, Pat. "Foster Care in Books for Children." *School Library Journal* 30 (Feb. 1984): 28–31.

Background

Paterson, Katherine. "Hope Is More than Happiness." (endings to stories for children) *New York Times Book Review* 93 (Dec. 25, 1988): 19.

Paterson, Katherine. "Living in a Peaceful World." (equipping children to grow toward wholeness and peace) *Horn Book* 67 (Jan./Feb. 1991): 32–38.

Paterson, Katherine. "People I Have Known." *The Writer* 100 (April 1987): 22–24.

Paterson, Katherine. *The Spying Heart: More Thoughts on Reading and Writing Books for Children.* New York: Lodestar Books, 1988.

Schmidt, Gary D. *Katherine Paterson.* New York: Twayne, 1993.

"Waxing Creative." (inspirations of children's authors and illustrators) *Publishers Weekly* 242 (July 17, 1995): 138–41.

Awards and Prizes

American Book Award, 1980

Garden State Children's Book Award for Younger Fiction from the New Jersey Library Association, 1981

Iowa Children's Choice Award from Iowa Educational Media Association, 1981

Jane Addams Peace Association Children's Book Award Honor Book, 1979

National Book Award for Children's Literature, 1979

Newbery Medal Honor Book, 1979

School Library Journal's Best Books of the Year, 1978

References about the Author

Children's Literature Review. Detroit: Gale, 1984. v. 7, pp. 224–43.

Contemporary Authors. Detroit: Gale, 1977. v. 21–24, p. 662.

Contemporary Authors, New Revision Series. Detroit: Gale, 1990. v. 28, pp. 359–64.

Contemporary Literary Criticism. Detroit: Gale, 1980. v. 30, pp. 283, 285, 287; v. 12, pp. 486–87.

Dictionary of Literary Biography. Detroit: Gale, 1986. v. 52, pp. 296–314.

Something about the Author. Detroit: Gale, 1988. v. 53, pp. 118–28; v. 13, pp. 176–77.

Sources Recommending This Book

Children's Catalog. 16th ed. Ed. Juliette Yaakov. New York: H. W. Wilson, 1991.

Colborn, Candy. *What Do Children Read Next? A Reader's Guide to Fiction for Children.* Detroit: Gale, 1994.

Gillespie, John T. *The Elementary School Paperback Collection.* Chicago: American Library Association, 1985.

Gillespie, John T. *The Junior High School Paperback Collection.* Chicago: American Library Association, 1985.

Gillespie, John T., and Christine Gilbert, eds. *Best Books for Children: Preschool through the Middle Grades.* 3rd ed. New York: R. R. Bowker, 1985.

*Junior High School Library Catalog.*16th ed. Ed. Juliette Yaakov. New York: H. W. Wilson, 1990.

Lee, Lauren K., ed. *The Elementary School Library Collection: A Guide to Books and Other Media.* 18th ed. Williamsport, Pa.: Brodart, 1992.

Middle and Junior High School Library Catalog. 7th ed. Ed. Anne Price and Juliette Yaakov. New York: H. W. Wilson, 1995.

The Young Adult Reader's Adviser: The Best in Social Sciences, History, Science and Health. Vol. 2. Ed. Myra Immell. New Providence, N.J.: R. R. Bowker, 1992.

Harry Potter and the Sorcerer's Stone

English title: Harry Potter and the Philosopher's Stone

New York: Scholastic/Arthur A. Levine, 1998

Harry Potter and the Chamber of Secrets

New York: Scholastic/Arthur A. Levine, 1999

Harry Potter and the Prisoner of Azkaban

New York: Scholastic/Arthur A. Levine, 1999

Harry Potter and the Goblet of Fire

New York: Scholastic/Arthur A. Levine, 2000

As he turns eleven, Harry is rescued from his miserable position in his aunt and uncle's household in these, the first four books (of a planned series of seven) chronicling his career at Hogwarts School of Witchcraft and Wizardry. The boy who slept in the cupboard below the stairs discovers that he is famous in the parallel world of the wizards, where he survives the attack of the evil Voldemort, his parents' murderer. At Hogwarts he not only learns potions, spells, and other magical musts, but also discovers friendship and community. He has enemies, too— those who envy his fame or would have Voldemort rise again.

Each of the books takes readers through one year of Harry's life, presenting him with a new set of dangers to be overcome. *Booklist* reviewer Sally Estes remarked on the continuity of the Harry Potter books, "with villains, heroes, schemers, and innocents all firmly in their places, the seemingly impossible solved, and good triumphing over evil."

J. K. Rowling was named Author of the Year in 2000 in the United Kingdom, where the books have won numerous prizes, including the Whitbread Children's Book of the Year and the Nestlé Smarties Book Prize. *Harry Potter and the Sorcerer's Stone* won the American Bookseller's Award in 1999.

Challenges

To challenge an individual Harry Potter book is to challenge the entire series, as the belief that wizardry is inherently evil is at the heart of most challenges. In 1999, this series, with three books in print, topped the list of most challenged books. In South Carolina, the series was challenged because the books have "a serious tone of death, hate, lack of respect, and sheer evil." Other challenges occurred in Douglas County, Colorado; Moorpark, California; and suburban Buffalo, New York.

The school superintendent in Zeeland, Michigan, ordered teachers to refrain from reading the books in class and permitted librarians to check them out only to students in grades five to eight who have written permission from parents; further, he said that the district would not purchase future books in the series. Several other districts in western Michigan followed suit.

Many challenges have brought out local defenders. In Lakeville, Minnesota, numerous parents rallied to the books' defense when other parents objected to the books being read in elementary school. In Saginaw, Michigan, the books were removed from a classroom because of a parent's religious objection, but the principal assured the school's other teachers that they were still free to use the books in their classes if they wished. In Frankfort, Illinois, parents asked the superintendent of schools to forbid teachers to read the books in class because they contained "lying and smart-aleck retorts to adults," but the superintendent chose instead to allow parents to remove their children from any reading sessions they deem inappropriate. The publicity over Harry Potter prompted a class of third-graders in Pelham, New York, to write letters in support of the books and to lead a forum against censorship.

Reviews

Harry Potter and the Sorcerer's Stone

Booklist 95 (Sept. 15, 1998): 230.

Bulletin of the Center for Children's Books 52 (Nov. 1998): 110.

Christian Science Monitor 91 (Jan. 14, 1999): 19.

Horn Book 75 (Jan./Feb. 1999): 71.

Kirkus Reviews 66 (Sept. 1, 1998): 1292.

New York Review of Books 46 (Dec. 16, 1999): 6.

Publishers Weekly 245 (July 20, 1998): 220.

School Library Journal 44 (Oct. 1998): 145.

Voice of Youth Advocates 22 (April 1999): 15.

Harry Potter and the Chamber of Secrets

Booklist 95 (May 15, 1999): 1690.

Bulletin of the Center for Children's Books 53 (Sept. 1999): 28.

Horn Book 75 (July/Aug. 1999): 472.

Kirkus Reviews 67 (June 1, 1999): 888.

Publishers Weekly 246 (May 31, 1999): 94.

School Library Journal 45 (July 1999): 99.

Voice of Youth Advocates 22 (Oct. 1999): 272.

Harry Potter and the Prisoner of Azkaban

Booklist 96 (Sept. 1, 1999): 127.

Bulletin of the Center for Children's Books 53 (Oct. 1999): 68.

Horn Book 75 (Nov./Dec. 1999): 744.

Kirkus Reviews 67 (Sept. 15, 1999): 1506.

Publishers Weekly 246 (July 19, 1999): 195.

School Library Journal 45 (Oct. 1999): 158.

Harry Potter and the Goblet of Fire

Horn Book 76 (Nov./Dec. 2000): 762–63.

New York Times Book Review, July 23, 2000, 13–14.

Newsweek, July 17, 2000, 52–56.

School Library Journal 46 (Aug. 2000): 188.

Background

Acocella, Joan. "Under the Spell." *New Yorker*, July 31, 2000, 74–78.

Blume, Judy. "Is Harry Potter Evil?" *New York Times,* Oct. 22, 1999, Sec. A.

Bouquet, Tim. "The Wizard Behind Harry Potter." *Reader's Digest,* December 2000, 95–101.

Carson, Tom. "Midnight's Children." *Village Voice,* July 25, 2000, 63.

Gray, Paul. "Wild about Harry." *Time,* Sept. 20, 1999, 67–72.

Zimmerman, Jonathan. "Harry Potter and His Censors." *Education Week* 19 (Aug. 2, 2000): 44

Awards and Prizes

Harry Potter and the Philosopher's Stone

British Book Award, Children's Book of the Year, 1997

Rowntree Nestlé Smarties Prize, 1997

Harry Potter and the Sorcerer's Stone

Rebecca Caudill Young Readers' Book Award, 2001

Harry Potter and the Chamber of Secrets

Rowntree Nestlé Smarties Prize, 1998

Harry Potter and the Prisoner of Azkaban

Whitbread Children's Book of the Year, 1999

Harry Potter and the Goblet of Fire

W. H. Smith Children's Book of the Year, 2000

Hugo Award for Best Novel, 2001

References about the Author

Children's Literature Review. Detroit: Gale, 2001. v. 66, pp. 77–111.

Contemporary Authors. Detroit: Gale, 1999. v. 173, pp. 376–78.

Something about the Author. Detroit: Gale, 2000. v. 109, pp. 199–202.

Sources Recommending This Series

Homa, Linda L. *The Elementary School Collection.* 22nd ed. Williamsport, Pa.: Brodart, 2000.

Price, Anne, and Juliette Yaakov, eds. *Middle and Junior High School Library Catalog.* 8th ed. New York: H. W. Wilson, 2000.

LOUIS SACHAR

The Boy Who Lost His Face

New York: Knopf, 1989

Wanting to be a member of the popular crowd, David joins Roger, Scott, and Randy in a cruel prank. They pretend to befriend old Mrs. Bayfield, who they think is a witch, and steal her cane, knock her and her rocking chair over, pour lemonade over her face, and throw the empty pitcher through a window. As they are running away from the crime scene, David flips off the old woman. She screams, and it sounds to David like a curse. David becomes convinced that Mrs. Bayfield did indeed put a curse on him because everything the boys did to her is now happening to him.

From the moment the crime is committed, David feels guilty about his part in it; he continually questions his behavior and toys with the idea of apologizing to Mrs. Bayfield. As he gains self-confidence and learns to trust his own judgment, David realizes that an apology to Mrs. Bayfield is necessary. When he does apologize to her, she asks him to get her cane back for her. David gets the cane back from Roger, even though a fight ensues. David thinks that the curse will be lifted when he returns the cane. But on his visit to give the cane back, he discovers that Mrs. Bayfield is not a witch, and she has not put a curse on him.

This contemporary, realistic novel accurately portrays the feelings of alienation, acceptance, love, and friendship experienced by young people as they travel through adolescence, which is a most difficult time in their lives.

Challenges

Removed from the Jackson Township Elementary School in Clay City, Indiana (1993), because of "unsuitable words."

Challenged at the Golden View Elementary School in San Ramon, California (1993), because of profanity, frequent use of obscene gestures, and other inappropriate subject matter.

Removed from the Cuyler Elementary School in Red Creek, New York (1993), because "the age level and use of some swear words may make it inappropriate to younger children."

Challenged at the Thousand Oaks, California, Library (1991) because of inappropriate language.

Reviews

Booklist 86 (Nov. 15, 1989): 675.

Children's Book Review Service 18 (Nov. 1989): 36.

Horn Book 1 (July 1989): 79.

References about the Author

Children's Literature Review. Detroit: Gale, 1992. v. 28, pp. 200–5.

Contemporary Authors. Detroit: Gale, 1979. v. 81–84, p. 491.

Contemporary Authors, New Revision Series. Detroit: Gale, 1991. v. 33, p. 386; v. 15, p. 389.

Something about the Author. Detroit: Gale, 1991. v. 63, pp. 137–40; v. 50, p. 188.

Scary Stories to Tell in the Dark

New York: HarperCollins, 1981

More Scary Stories to Tell in the Dark

New York: HarperCollins, 1984

Scary Stories 3: More Tales to Chill Your Bones

New York: HarperCollins, 1991

Each of these three books draws on folk-lore—old tales and urban legends—as the basis for ghost stories, verses, and songs that send chills down the spine. Stephen Gammell's black-and-white illustrations, liberally scattered throughout all three books, have the right balance of realism and malevolence to sustain the books' eerie atmosphere.

Some of the tales depend on delivery for maximum effect, and Schwartz has included tips for telling. ("As you shout the last words, stamp your foot and jump at someone nearby.") The end of some stories is humorous or perfectly logical, while others have an ending that can only be explained through the supernatural. The first book contains six pages of source notes for the tales and a bibliography that includes both the sources and books for further reading. In the two sequels, the notes and source information are even more detailed. Reviewers at *School Library Journal* have welcomed all three of these books, noting that they are "well-suited for children" and "well-used addition[s] to all collections."

Challenges

All three books

Removed from Vancouver, Washington, School District school libraries in 1994 after surviving two previous attempts in 1991 and 1993.

Challenged at the Lake Washington School District in Kirkland, Washington, in 1992 as unacceptably violent for children.

Scary Stories to Tell in the Dark

Restricted to students in the fourth grade or higher in Enfield, Connecticut, elementary school libraries in 1995.

Challenged at Happy Valley Elementary School in Glasgow, Kentucky, in 1993 by a parent who thought it was too scary.

Access restricted at the Marana, Arizona, Unified School District in 1993 because of complaints about violence and cannibalism.

Challenged at the elementary school library in Union County, Indiana, in 1992.

Challenged at the West Hartford, Connecticut, elementary and middle-school libraries in 1992 because of violence and the subject matter.

Challenged at the Neely Elementary School in Gilbert, Arizona, in 1992 because the book shows the dark side of religion through the occult, the devil, and Satanism.

More Scary Stories to Tell in the Dark

Challenged, but retained, as part of a district reading list in Harper Woods, Michigan, in 1995.

Unsuccessfully challenged at the Whittier Elementary School Library in Bozeman, Montana, in 1994 on the grounds it would cause children to fear the dark and have nightmares, and would give them an unrealistic view of death.

Access restricted at the Marana, Arizona, Unified School District in 1993 because of complaints about violence and cannibalism.

Challenged at the Neely Elementary School in Gilbert, Arizona, in 1992 because the book shows the dark side of religion through the occult, the devil, and Satanism.

Scary Stories 3

Challenged at the West Hartford, Connecticut, elementary and middle-school libraries in 1992 because of violence and the subject matter.

Reviews

Scary Stories to Tell in the Dark

Booklist 78 (Dec. 15, 1981): 552.

Bulletin of the Center for Children's Books 35 (June 1982): 198.

Horn Book 58 (Feb. 1982): 58.

School Library Journal 28 (Jan. 1982): 81.

More Scary Stories to Tell in the Dark

Booklist 81 (March 1, 1985): 989.

Bulletin of the Center for Children's Books 38 (Feb. 1985): 116.

Horn Book 61 (Feb. 1985): 183.

School Library Journal 31 (Feb. 1985): 801.

Voice of Youth Advocates 8 (April 1985): 51.

Scary Stories 3

Booklist 87 (Aug. 1991): 2146.

Bulletin of the Center for Children's Books 45 (Dec. 1991): 105.

Horn Book 67 (Nov. 1991): 749.

Publishers Weekly 238 (Aug. 9, 1991): 58.

Background

Jones, Patrick. "Have No Fear: Scary Stories for the Middle Grades." *Emergency Librarian* 21 (Sept./Oct. 1993): 30–32.

Schwartz, Alvin. "Children, Humor and Folklore." *Catholic Library World* 59 (Sept./Oct. 1987): 67–70.

Zvirin, Stephanie. "Before Stephen King." *Booklist* 91 (Jan. 1, 1995): 830–31.

References about the Author

Children's Literature Review. Detroit: Gale, 1978. v. 3, pp. 187–93.

Contemporary Authors. Detroit: Gale, 1975. v. 13–16, p. 709.

Contemporary Authors, New Revision Series. Detroit: Gale, 1992. v. 137, p. 405; v. 24, pp. 419–21; v. 7, pp. 431–32.

Something about the Author. Detroit: Gale, 1993. v. 71, p. 171; v. 56, pp. 145–51; v. 4, pp. 183–84.

Sources Recommending These Books

Gillespie, John T. *Best Books for Children: Preschool through Grade Six.* 6th ed. New York: R. R. Bowker, 1998.

Gillespie, John T. *Best Books for Junior High Readers.* New Providence, N.J.: R. R. Bowker, 1991.

Homa, Linda L., ed. *The Elementary School Library Collection: A Guide to Books and Other Media.* 22nd ed. Williamsport, Pa.: Brodart, 2000.

Price, Anne, and Juliette Yaakov. *Children's Catalog.* 17th ed. New York: H. W. Wilson, 1996.

MAURICE SENDAK

In the Night Kitchen

New York: Harper and Row, 1970

In a dream, Mickey floats through the night sky, arriving at the Night Kitchen. He lands in a bowl of unfinished cake batter. Mistaking Mickey for the final ingredient—milk—the three bakers continue stirring the batter. Mickey then skips into a batch of rising bread dough. After kneading it to baking consistency, Mickey makes an airplane out of the mixture. He flies up into the night sky, tumbles out of the airplane, and falls into a giant milk bottle. Mickey pours some milk into the unfinished cake batter. The bakers are delighted that they've finally been given the missing ingredient. They mix the batter, beat the batter, and put it in the oven to bake. By daybreak, Mickey is back in his own bed—asleep, "cakefree and dried." He wakes up knowing how he is able to have "cake every morning" for breakfast.

This surrealistic fantasy-dream is set against a clever and imaginative city skyline that has been built using a wide variety of cooking utensils and kitchen containers, including jars, cartons, cans, boxes, and even salt and pepper shakers.

The perfect combination of a text based in the literary tradition of nursery rhymes and illustrations executed in a 1930-ish, art-deco style evokes the comforting smells and decor of a homey, family kitchen.

Although acclaimed by many, this picture book initially was received with cries of outrage because of Sendak's blatant use of nudity and exploration of a child's sexuality.

Since the book was first published, "concerned" librarians, teachers, and parents have taken the liberty of dressing Mickey in diapers or pants by drawing over pictures of his unclothed body.

Certainly ahead of its time, this early work of Sendak's remains a favorite of children.

Challenges

Challenged at the El Paso, Texas, Public Library (1994) because "the little boy pictured did not have any clothes on and it pictured his private area."

Because reading the book "could lay the foundation for future use of pornography," the book was challenged at the Elk River, Minnesota, schools in 1992.

Challenged at the Camden, New Jersey, elementary school libraries because of nudity in 1989.

Challenged at the Robeson Elementary School in Champaign, Illinois (1988), because of "gratuitous" nudity.

Reviews

Booklist 67 (Jan. 15, 1971): 423.

Bulletin of the Center for Children's Books 24 (Jan. 1971): 80.

Horn Book 47 (Feb. 1971): 44.

Library Journal 95 (Dec. 15, 1970): 4341.

Articles about This Book

Elswit, Sharon. "Bedtime Books for Bedtime." *School Library Journal* 26 (March 1980): 104–5.

Background

Nickerson, Mary. "Princess Moaning Minnie, Mrs. Coalsack, and Muggle-Wump Meet Randy Monroe." *School Library Journal* 27 (Oct. 1980): 118–19.

Sadler, Glen Edward. "Maurice Sendak and Dr. Seuss: A Conversation." *Horn Book* 65 (Sept./Oct. 1989): 582–88.

Sendak, Maurice. "The Coming Together of All My Various Worlds." *Top of the News* 26 (June 1970): 366–69.

Awards and Prizes

Art Books for Children Award, 1973, 1974, and 1975

Caldecott Medal Honor Book, 1971

Chandler Book Talk Reward of Merit, 1967

Hans Christian Andersen Award, for body of his illustration work, 1970

Notable Children's Book, 1970

Redbook Award, 1985

School Library Journal's Best Books of the Year, 1970

References about the Author

Children's Literature Review. Detroit: Gale, 1989. v. 17, pp. 93–129; v. 1, pp. 166–73.

Contemporary Authors. Detroit: Gale, 1969. v. 5–8, p. 1035.

Contemporary Authors, New Revision Series. Detroit: Gale, 1992. v. 39, pp. 354–61; v. 11, pp. 457–65.

Something about the Author. Detroit: Gale, 1982. v. 27, pp. 181–201; v. 1, pp. 190–91.

Sources Recommending This Book

Children's Catalog. 16th ed. Ed. Juliette Yaakov. New York: H. W. Wilson, 1991.

Donavin, Denise Perry. *Best of the Best for Children.* Chicago: American Library Association, 1992.

Gillespie, John T., and Christine Gilbert, eds. *Best Books for Children: Preschool through the Middle Grades.* 3rd ed. New York: R. R. Bowker, 1985.

Lee, Lauren K., ed. *The Elementary School Library Collection: A Guide to Books and Other Media.* 18th ed. Williamsport, Pa.: Brodart, 1992.

Sutherland, Zena. *The Best in Children's Books.* Chicago: University of Chicago Press, 1991.

A Light in the Attic

New York: Harper and Row, 1981

In this witty, original collection of poems by the author of the ever-popular *Where the Sidewalk Ends,* young readers meet a cast of interesting, wacky characters and read about many unusual, strange happenings. The poems vary in length, style, and humor. As in Silverstein's other work, stark line drawings complement the poems wonderfully.

A few of the poems revisit familiar nursery rhymes, such as "Rockabye," in which the narrator questions why anyone would put a baby and its cradle in a treetop. Spin-offs of well-known fairy tales are evident in several poems, including "Picture Puzzle Piece," "Captain Blackbeard Did What?" and "In Search of Cinderella." Children will definitely relate to their peers in such poems as "How Not to Have to Dry the Dishes," "Prayer of a Selfish Child," and "Little Abigail and the Beautiful Pony." Some poems, including "Whatifs" and "The Little Boy and the Old Man," explore the more sensitive feelings of children, but most of the poems are downright silly and nonsensical. The collection is perfect for reading aloud and will tickle the funny bones of young listeners and readers alike.

Some parents have questioned the irreverent subjects addressed in some of the poems, including a babysitter who sits on the baby she's caring for and damsels who are eaten by the Dragon of Grindly Grun. Others have objected to the nudity shown in several illustrations, people drowning, bodies with missing parts, a child's death because her parents refused to buy her a pony, and possible disrespect to God.

In spite of parental concern about these and other poems that are anthologized in this book, *A Light in the Attic* has vast child-appeal. Professional book reviewers have praised this entertaining and humorous poetry collection. Since its publication in 1981, because of the book's immense popularity and the high demand from youngsters everywhere, libraries across the country rarely have had copies of this book sitting on shelves.

Challenges

Challenged, but retained, on the Webb City, Missouri, school library shelves (1996). A parent had protested that the book imparts a "dreary" and "negative" message.

Challenged at the Fruitland Park Elementary School Library in Lake County, Florida (1993), because the book "promotes disrespect, horror, and violence."

Because the poem "Little Abigail and the Beautiful Pony" is morbid, the book was challenged at the West Mifflin, Pennsylvania, schools in 1992.

Restricted to students with parental permission at the Duval County, Florida, public school libraries (1992) because the book features a caricature of a person whose nude behind has been stung by a bee.

Challenged at the South Adams, Indiana, school libraries (1989) because the book is "very vile" and "contained subliminal or underlying messages and anti-parent material."

Challenged as suitable classroom material because of its "objectionable" nature at the Hot Springs, South Dakota, Elementary School in 1989.

Because a mother protested that it "exposes children to the horrors of suicide," the poem "Little Abigail and the Beautiful Pony," from this award-winning children's book, was banned from second-grade classes in Huffman, Texas, in 1989.

Challenged at the Morneo Valley, California, Unified School District libraries (1987) because it "contains profanity, sexual situations, and themes that allegedly encourage disrespectful behavior."

Challenged at the Appoquinimink schools in Middletown, Delaware (1987), because the book "contains violence, idealizes death, and makes light of manipulative behavior."

Reviews

Booklist 78 (Dec. 1, 1981): 502.

Bulletin of the Center for Children's Books 35 (Feb. 1982): 117.

Catholic Library World 53 (March 1982): 357.

Kirkus Reviews 50 (Jan. 1, 1982): 10.

Publishers Weekly 220 (Sept. 18, 1981): 155.

School Librarian 31 (March 1983): 73.

School Library Journal 28 (Dec. 1981): 57.

School Library Media Quarterly 10 (spring 1982): 206.

Voice of Youth Advocates 4 (Feb. 1982): 45.

Background

Livingston, Myra Cohn. "The Light in His Attic." (work of S. Silverstein) *New York Times Book Review* 91 (March 9, 1986): 36–37.

Wallace, Robert. "Light Verse." *The Writer* 98 (Dec. 1985): 20–22.

Awards and Prizes

Buckeye Award, 1983 and 1985

George G. Stone Award, 1984

Notable Children's Recording, 1986

School Library Journal's Best Books of the Year, 1981

William Allen White Award, 1984

References about the Author

Children's Literature Review. Detroit: Gale, 1983. v. 5, pp. 208–13.

Contemporary Authors. Detroit: Gale, 1983. v. 107, pp. 471–72.

Contemporary Authors, New Revision Series. Detroit: Gale, 1995. v. 47, pp. 403–5.

Something about the Author. Detroit: Gale, 1983. v. 33, pp. 210–13; v. 27, p. 202.

Sources Recommending This Book

"Books to Make You Giggle and Grin." *Emergency Librarian* 12 (May/June 1985): 11–12.

Children's Catalog. 16th ed. Ed. Juliette Yaakov. New York: H. W. Wilson, 1991.

Donavin, Denise Perry. *Best of the Best for Children.* Chicago: American Library Association, 1992.

Gillespie, John T., ed. *Best Books for Junior High Readers*. New Providence, N.J.: R. R. Bowker, 1991.

Gillespie, John T., and Christine Gilbert, eds. *Best Books for Children: Preschool through the Middle Grades*. 3rd ed. New York: R. R. Bowker, 1985.

Junior High School Library Catalog. 16th ed. Ed. Juliette Yaakov. New York: H. W. Wilson, 1990.

Lee, Lauren K., ed. *The Elementary School Library Collection: A Guide to Books and Other Media*. 18th ed. Williamsport, Pa.: Brodart, 1992.

Middle and Junior High School Library Catalog. 7th ed. Ed. Anne Price and Juliette Yaakov. New York: H. W. Wilson, 1995.

Goosebumps

New York: Scholastic

The original Goosebumps series was inaugurated in 1992 with *Welcome to Dead House* (#1) and concluded in 1997 with *Monster Blood IV* (#62). As each new book was published, it immediately moved onto the children's best-selling paperback lists, and sales figures per book often reached one million copies and beyond. Spin-offs from the original series are *Goosebumps Presents,* a tie-in to the television show, and *Give Yourself Goosebumps,* a choose-your-own-ending series. In 1998, Goosebumps 2000 replaced the original Goosebumps series and the numbering began once again with #1.

The books in the Goosebumps series do not share the same cast of characters or setting, but all pull from the same bag of tricks: fast action, cliffhangers at the end of each chapter, and unrealistic plots. The characters do not grow in the books, nor do the books pretend to be art. The books are geared to readers between eight and twelve and cater to their delight in anything gross, disgusting, and creepy. In an interview with *Publishers Weekly,* Stine has said that he sees these books as entertainment and tries to keep reality out of them. "The real world is much scarier than these books. So I don't do divorce, even. I don't do drugs. I don't do child abuse. I don't do all the really serious things that would interfere with the entertainment."

Instead, the author marries ordinary kids and situations with supernatural events, usually telling the story in the first person and ending the book in a way that sometimes defies logic. In his biography of R. L. Stine, Patrick Jones noted, "Part of the appeal of Stine's books is that they read like stories that are told rather than written. The easy vocabulary, short sentences, and conversational style give Goosebumps a campfire scary story feel."

Challenges

Through early 1997, ALA was informed of forty-six challenges involving the entire series or individual Goosebumps titles. More than 75 percent of these challenges occurred in school library settings, while the remaining challenges were to books held in public libraries or could not be pinpointed. When a challenge is not reported to ALA but is picked up by the media, it is not always clear whether the challenged book is part of a school or public library collection.

In Minneapolis, Minnesota, a mother requested that nine Goosebumps titles be banned from the school district in 1997, citing them as "too frightening for children and inappropriate for school libraries." The book review committee, composed of school employees and parents, voted to retain the books. The controversy

58 ■ GOOSEBUMPS

prompted more than four hundred letters from district residents, and ninety people, including some children, testified at the two hearings.

In Bay County, Florida, the entire series was challenged (1996), with passages from five books cited as examples of satanic symbolism, demonic possession, and violence. The school board voted to keep the books in school libraries, to allow teachers the right to choose books to read to their classes, and to give parents the right to request alternative assignments.

In Parks, Arizona, a parent complaint to the school superintendent resulted in a policy that removed the books from school library shelves and restricted their checkout to students in grades three through six (1996).

Background

McGillis, Roderick. "R. L. Stine and the World of Child Gothic." *Bookbird* 33 (fall/winter 1995–1996): 15–21.

Stine, R. L. "Lurking in the Dark." *Newsweek* (Nov. 2, 1998): 66.

Wargo, Suzanne, and Alberta Graham. "Should Kids Read Goosebumps?" *NEA Today* 16 (Oct. 1997): 43.

References about the Author

Alderdice, Kit. "R. L. Stine: 90 Million Spooky Adventures." *Publishers Weekly* 242 (July 17, 1995): 208–9.

Children's Literature Review. Detroit: Gale, 1996. v. 37, pp. 101–23.

Contemporary Authors, New Revision Series. Detroit: Gale, 1997. v. 53, pp. 452–56.

Jones, Patrick. *What's So Scary about R. L. Stine?* Lanham, Md.: Scarecrow, 1998.

Something about the Author. Detroit: Gale, 1994. v. 76, pp. 219–24.

Daddy's Roommate

Boston: Alyson Publications, 1990

Daddy's Roommate, a picture book for young readers, is told from the perspective of a young boy who spends time with his father and his father's partner, Frank, following the divorce of his parents. The two men are portrayed as a loving couple in a realistic way—they "work together, eat together, sleep together, shave together, and sometimes even fight together, but they always make up."

The child tells us about Frank, his father's roommate, showing how much fun they have. He also describes the things the three of them do when they are together.

Just as the two men are seen to relate to one another like any other couple, the adventures that the young boy has with Daddy and Frank are the same as any other child might have. When his mother explains that the child's father and Frank love each other, and that is why they live together, the boy responds: "Being gay is just one more kind of love, and love is the best kind of happiness." The boy closes the book with the observation that "Daddy and his roommate are very happy together, and I'm happy too!"

Because the book does a good job expressing the humanity and "normality" of gay people, it is a good choice for schools and libraries wishing to include in their collections books that encourage understanding and confront misconceptions about gays and lesbians.

Unfortunately, the critical success of the book also raised its visibility, resulting in more challenges, removals, and reclassifications.

Daddy's Roommate is suited perfectly to its audience, using simple language and bold illustrations to tell the story. As such, it is an effective means by which children can get a glimpse of the truth of mainstream gay life without fear or suspicion. The book is important as well for children who have gay parents—not only does it reflect their own lives, which is always important and empowering, but also it can serve as a catalyst for dialogue between these children and their peers. *Daddy's Roommate* expresses beautifully that gay people can love as well and parent as well as anyone else, in a manner that is entirely appropriate to its audience.

Challenges

Challenged, but retained, in the juvenile nonfiction section of the Nampa, Idaho, Public Library (1999).

Challenged at the Wichita Falls, Texas, Public Library (1998). The deacon body of the First Baptist Church requested that any literature that promotes or sanctions a homosexual lifestyle be removed. The Wichita Falls City Council established a policy that allows library card holders who collect three hundred signatures to have children's books moved to an adult section of the library. U.S. District Court Judge Jerry Buchmeyer struck down the library resolution as unconstitutional, and the books were returned.

Challenged, but retained, at the Hays, Kansas, Public Library (1998). A resident objected to "the teaching of the homosexual lifestyle as another way to show love."

Challenged at the Brevard County, Florida, Library (1998). When a request to ban the book failed, the complainant kept the book from other patrons by keeping it checked out for a year.

After more than a month of controversy and debate, trustees of the Rutland, Vermont, Free Library decided, in 1995, not to create a special section for or restrict access to the book.

Removed from the children's section of the Fort Worth, Texas, Public Library (1994) because critics said it legitimizes gay relationships.

Challenged at the Chandler, Arizona, Public Library (1994) because the book is a "skillful presentation to the young child about lesbianism/homosexuality."

Removed by Land County Head Start officials in Cottage Grove, Oregon, from its anti-bias curriculum in 1994.

Challenged, but retained, at the Dayton and Montgomery County, Ohio, Public Library in 1993.

Because it is "vile, sick and goes against every law and constitution," the book was challenged at the Mesa, Arizona, Public Library in 1993.

Challenged at the Alachua County Library in High Springs, Florida, in 1993.

Challenged at the Seekonk, Massachusetts, Library in 1993.

Challenged at the North Brunswick, New Jersey, Public Library in 1993.

Challenged at the Cumberland County, North Carolina, Public Library in 1993.

Challenged at the Chattanooga–Hamilton County, Tennessee, Bicentennial Library in 1993.

Challenged at the Wicomico County Free Library in Salisbury, Maryland, in 1993.

Challenged at the Sussex, Wisconsin, Public Library in 1993.

Challenged at the Juneau, Alaska, school libraries in 1993.

Moved from the children's section to the adult section at the Manatee, Florida, Public Library in 1993, and the Elizabethtown, North Carolina, library, also in 1993.

Restricted to adults at the Lake Lamer Regional Library System in Gwinnett County, Georgia, in 1993.

Moved from the children's section to the adult section of the Mercer County Library System in Lawrence, New Jersey, in 1993.

Challenged in the Rosemount Apple Valley School District in Eden, Minnesota, in 1993.

Because it "promotes a dangerous and ungodly lifestyle from which children must be protected," the book was challenged in the Wayne County Public Library in Goldsboro, North Carolina; the Grand Prairie, Texas, Memorial Library; the Cumberland County Public Library, Fayetteville, North Carolina; and the Tillamook, Oregon, Public Library in 1992.

Challenged (in 1992) at the Roswell Public Library in New Mexico and the Dauphin County Library System in Pennsylvania because the book's intent "is indoctrination into a gay lifestyle."

Challenged at the Timberland Regional Libraries in Olympia, Washington (1992), because the book promotes homosexuality and is offensive.

Removed from the Brooklyn, New York, School District's curriculum (1992) because the school board objected to words that were "age inappropriate."

Reviews

Booklist 87 (March 1, 1991): 1403.

Bulletin of the Center for Children's Books 44 (March 1991): 182.

Publishers Weekly 237 (Dec. 7, 1990): 80.

School Library Journal 37 (April 1991): 105.

Articles about This Book

Loch, Marge Wouters. "Children's Cornucopia: Whose Family's Values?

Gay and Lesbian Families in Children's Books." *WLW Journal* 15 (winter 1992/1993): 13–14.

Background

Ford, Michael Thomas. "Gay Books for Young Readers: When Caution Calls the Shots." *Publishers Weekly* 241 (Feb. 21, 1994): 24–27.

References about the Author

Something about the Author. Detroit: Gale, 1993. v. 71, pp. 213–15.

What ALA Can Do to Help Librarians Combat Censorship

The American Library Association maintains a broad program for the promotion and defense of intellectual freedom. Its various components include the Intellectual Freedom Committee (IFC), which recommends policy to the ALA Council and sponsors educational programs; the Office for Intellectual Freedom (OIF), which implements ALA policy concerning the concept of intellectual freedom as embodied in the *Library Bill of Rights;* the Intellectual Freedom Round Table, which provides the opportunity for ALA members to become involved in the promotion and defense of intellectual freedom; and the Intellectual Freedom Action Network, which is comprised of volunteers who have expressed a willingness to support the freedom to read in censorship controversies in their communities.

The basic program of the Intellectual Freedom Committee is educational in nature. The most effective safeguards for the rights of library users and librarians are an informed public and a library profession aware of repressive activities and how to combat them. Toward this end, the administrative arm of the Intellectual Freedom Committee, the Office for Intellectual Freedom, implements ALA policies on intellectual freedom and educates librarians about the importance of the concept. The Office for Intellectual Freedom maintains a wide-ranging program of educational and informational publications, projects, and services.

One of the Intellectual Freedom Committee's most important publications is the bimonthly *Newsletter on Intellectual Freedom (NIF)*. The *NIF* was initiated in 1952 and has been edited and produced by the OIF staff since 1970. The *NIF* is addressed to both librarians and the general public concerned about intellectual freedom. It provides a comprehensive, national picture of censorship efforts, court cases, legislation, and current readings on the subject. Through original and reprinted articles, the *NIF* offers a forum for expressing varying views about intellectual freedom while providing a means for reporting activities of the IFC, the OIF, and the Freedom to Read Foundation. In 1982, noted civil liberties authority Nat Hentoff named the *NIF* "the best small publication

---

Adopted in part from the *Intellectual Freedom Manual*, 6th ed., by the Office for Intellectual Freedom (American Library Association, 2001).

in America." Additional information about the *NIF* can be found at www.ala. org/alaorg/oif/nif_inf.html. It is available by subscription from the OIF (1-800-545-2433, ext. 4223; oif@ala.org).

The office produces and distributes documents and articles concerning intellectual freedom to both librarians and the general public. Monographs, resource guides, training materials, and manuals include the *Intellectual Freedom Manual,* 6th edition; *Banned Books Week Resource Kit* (www.ala.org/bbooks/ resource.html); *Confidentiality in Libraries: An Intellectual Freedom Modular Education Program;* and *Censorship and Selection: Issues and Answers for Schools,* 3rd edition, by Henry Reichman (http://alastore.ala.org/). During nationwide controversies concerning individual titles, press clippings, editorials, and public statements detailing the ways various libraries around the country handled requests to remove specific materials are compiled and sent out to others dealing with similar problems.

One of the most often used and least heard about functions of the OIF is its provision of advice and consultation (case support) to individuals in the throes of potential or actual censorship controversies. Rarely does a day go by without the OIF receiving a request for assistance with a challenge to library materials. The OIF provides reviews and information about the author of the challenged material, applicable ALA policies, advice about the implementation of reconsideration policies, and other counseling specific to the situation at hand. If needed, the OIF will provide a written position statement defending the principles of intellectual freedom in materials selection. As requested, the OIF provides the names of persons available to offer testimony or support before library boards, supplied from the ranks of the Intellectual Freedom Action Network and state library association intellectual freedom committees. The options chosen are always the prerogative of the individual requesting assistance.

When a censorship problem arises, librarians have at least three options. They can visit "Dealing with Challenges to Books and Other Library Materials" (www.ala.org/alaorg/oif/dealingwithchallenges.html), on which is found links to materials to help cope with challenges; they can visit "Reporting a Challenge" (www.ala.org/alaorg/oif/reporting.html), on which is found links and information on who to contact regarding a challenge; or they can contact directly the Office for Intellectual Freedom (50 East Huron Street, Chicago, Illinois 60611; phone: 1-800-545-2433, ext. 4223; oif@ala.org).

See also "What You Can Do" (www.ala.org/alaorg/oif/whatyoucando.html), a list of suggestions on how to combat censorship. This list is published as part of the ALAAction series brochure, No. 2, *Intellectual Freedom* (www.ala.org/ alaorg/oif/ifbrochure.html) available from the ALA Public Information Office (1-800-545-2433, ext. 5041/5044; pio@ala.org; www.ala.org/pio). The online version of the list also includes links to information on intellectual freedom issues, intellectual freedom advocates, how to counter censorship in your community, how to celebrate your freedom to read, how to subscribe to various news and discussion e-lists, how to contact elected officials about issues and legislation related to intellectual freedom, and where to find news sources on intellectual freedom topics.

Over several decades, ALA and the library community as a whole have built an impressive network of support for intellectual freedom. The foundation of this network is the efforts of volunteer librarians, library trustees, and library users at the state and local levels. Such people have contributed and continue to contribute to the cause of intellectual freedom in many ways and through many organizational forms.

Combating censorship is never ending. To cope with challenges to library materials, librarians and the general public interested in defending and preserving intellectual freedom must be able to deal effectively with the media and to communicate effectively with concerned parents and would-be censors, who may be well organized and well financed. The best line of defense is good preparation, effective policies, knowing where to go for help when necessary, and library advocacy. The promotion of intellectual freedom and the promotion of libraries are inseparable.

Susan M. Stan is assistant professor at Central Michigan University, where she teaches courses in children's and young adult literature.

Beverley C. Becker is associate director of the Office for Intellectual Freedom of the American Library Association.